I0098790

WRITINGS

WRITINGS

~ † ~

JAMES THOMAS ANGELIDIS

Writings

James Thomas Angelidis

www.jtangelidis.com

First published by James Thomas Angelidis 2016.
This second edition published (as it appears in
Approaching the Kingdom: An Anthology)
by James Thomas Angelidis 2017.

Cover Design:
Layout by James Thomas Angelidis.

Author Image:
(On author bio page) Photograph taken of self by
James Thomas Angelidis.

AUTHOR BIO

James Thomas Angelidis has been awarded three university degrees and has authored and independently published several Christian books. These accomplishments helped him become a Professor of Christian Theology at Seton Hall University in South Orange, New Jersey. Discover James's works on his website at www.jtangelidis.com.

ABOUT

I believe there is truth in the proverb, "The pen is mightier than the sword."

The damage done by the emperor's sword can be rectified by the writer's pen. Nothing can replace a life lost by the sword, but with the help of the pen, the story of that life can teach, inspire and unveil truth that can save many lives. When the emperor dies, so does his sword, as does his power and his influence on the world; yet, the writer's pen can leave a lasting impression unto the ages. The ideas behind the pen can change the world; something, the emperor tries to do with his sword, but inevitably fails. Certainly, if we dig deeper, we can discover additional meanings within the proverb's words, but it is clear that the pen is powerful. The pen can make a difference in people's lives and with the help of God, I hope to make a difference in people's lives with my pen. I hope to give life.

- James Thomas Angelidis

CONTENTS

A THEOLOGICAL MEMOIR

JAMES THOMAS ANGELIDIS

The following is an article about my journey through the six great world religions' sacred scriptures.

After I graduated from the university, I moved back to my hometown and spent the next few summer months with friends. Up until this phase in my life, there was structure in my life that was as predictable as the seasons in a year. Since I was five years old, I had gone to school every year. Summer would arrive, then pass and school would begin, again. However, this year, after summer passed, my routine changed because school was over. At first, it was liberating. Few things are as sweet as graduating from a university. All that hard work is certified: you have accomplished something. The future is wide open and all things seem possible. However, as the months passed and I could not find a job, I realized things would not be as easy as I thought they would be.

After school, the next step is to get a job, but that next step is easier said than done. The economy was poor which made my task difficult and when I did have interviews, I was telling my potential employers what I thought they wanted to hear, but I had a tough time convincing them I was passionate about the work because I was not. I just wanted a job. For a while, I felt lost. The direction I was heading towards was not leading to anything. I had few "connections" that could have led to a "job." Though I was not "working," I began to make connections in my mind of how I saw the world. I used the information I learned in school and early on in the "real world" little by little, I made connections regarding money and success and aspirations. Relationships appeared and I began to formulate in my mind an idea of the life I wanted to lead.

The next two years of my life are difficult to clearly describe. There was little structure. I was working, but I had little direction. I eventually found work at a marketing department of a law firm in New York City, but this was a temporary job that only lasted for a few months. I had various jobs around town. I painted for a while and even considered making a career out of it, but I was not very sure of how to start a business. I even worked as an electrician's helper for a week. My most substantial job lasted for about one year. I was a laborer at an airline cargo warehouse. It was all manual labor, but I did not mind. It was a simple job. I put in my hours and got paid. I would finish my day then go home and eat dinner. It was honest work. I knew I had potential, but things were moving slowly. This period of my life lasted for about two years, but most of the real work was done in my bedroom with my books in my parent's house as I was coming to know God. It would be a very intense two years with great highs and great lows as I tried to figure out what was real and not fake, true and not false.

I read extensively and intensely after university. Many of the ideas and philosophies that I was introduced to in my liberal arts classes, I used to help me navigate through the "real world." And, that was the true value of my university education. What I learned in those liberal arts classes, I applied to my life. As students, we were not expected to be experts on anything, but be aware of the people, events and literature that changed the world, so we, too, could contribute to the world.

My interest in philosophy matured into a passion for religion in my search for truth. I forced myself to read - I learned how to read - not as a means to get a grade in a class, but for knowledge and wisdom that would help to create a foundation from which I could build my life. It started off little, like reading before bed. Then, it became a habit and I read every night before bed and each night I read more than the previous night. Sometimes, I would read at my desk, but I usually read facing down in my bed. Beside my bed, books piled and piled and were stacked one on top of another. I made sure they were always near me in case I changed direction in thought or needed to confirm some knowledge. I was an active reader taking notes and saving pages, so I could go back to the information that I found valuable and relearn it. This way, it would remain with me. The more I was reading, the more I was learning and the more I wanted to learn. I was hungry for knowledge and sometimes, I wanted to physically consume the books as if, with every swallow, the answers would come to me more quickly.

Every day for two years, I took a literary journey into the greatest literature that has ever been written. I journeyed through the great world religions' sacred scriptures. Below, I have displayed the concepts and beliefs that I find most provocative. I studied all the major religions. I learned that the great world religions can be classified into two types: those that come from human inquiry and those that are God attributed. Hinduism, Taoism and Buddhism are mainly the result of human inquiry and Judaism, Christianity and Islam are God attributed. I spent day and night learning about God and His ways and I felt closer to Him than ever before. Reading those amazing books was like finding treasure. There were nights that I could barely sit still because I was so elated by the jewels of wisdom and theology revealed in those sacred texts.

At the time, I was not a proactive participant in my faith. I was raised a Christian and never considered conversion to any other faith, but I was open to each faith. I never judged the religions and I was eager to examine each of them. My focus was in their sacred scriptures. I never stepped into a church or temple or mosque looking for answers and I never considered traditions or holidays. None of that ever occurred to me. Maybe, I was naive. But, I was hungry for knowledge and I knew I would find that knowledge in the scriptures. I dove into the scriptures themselves and not secondary literature. I wanted to know what made the religions they preached so powerful and why people lived and died for those religions.

I began my search with the religions that come from human inquiry. I was drawn to them because they were philosophical and because their sacred scriptures were short - their size was appealing. I learned that though their pages were minimal, they were potent.

Hinduism

For Hinduism, I studied the *Bhagavad-Gita* and the *Upanishads*. Of all the literature I examined during my journey, the Hindu *Bhagavad-Gita* was my favorite. I studied two different translations and read each translation completely at least twice and I referred back to the texts many times. I was first introduced to the *Bhagavad-Gita* during my studies at the university. Though I did not fully understand it when I was in school, I realized its importance once I began my investigation into eternal truths. It is life changing and life enhancing revelation. It is a spiritual warrior's guide and instruction manual to reach union with God. It teaches asceticism and mysticism. Chapters include: spiritual discipline, discipline of action, knowledge, infinite spirit, sublime mystery. It is also referred to as *Krishna's Council in Time of War.* In it, Lord Krishna councils Warrior-Prince Arjuna on how to transcend earthly desires and fight the spiritual battle within him, the same spiritual battle that takes place in each of us. Most inspiring is when Krishna tells Arjuna to:

> Look to your own duty;
> do not tremble before it;
> nothing is better for a warrior
> than a battle of sacred duty.

> The doors of heaven open
> for warriors who rejoice
> to have a battle like this
> thrust on them by chance.

> If you fail to wage this war
> of sacred duty,
> you will abandon your own duty

and fame only to gain evil.

People will tell
of your undying shame,
and for a man of honor
shame is worse than death.

The great chariot warriors will think
you deserted in fear of battle;
you will be despised
by those who held you in esteem.

Your enemies will slander you,
scorning your skill
in so many unspeakable ways -
could any suffering be worse?

If you are killed, you win heaven;
if you triumph, you enjoy the earth;
therefore, Arjuna, stand up
and resolve to fight the battle!

- *The Bhagavad-Gita*, 2.31-37
(Translation B.S. Miller)

I feel compelled and believe I have the
responsibility to emphasize and make clear that these
words of encouragement are for a spiritual battle that
takes place in one's soul and not a physical war with
weapons. I know that those inclined to read my story

are, most likely, not war minded, but I stress that this speech does not encourage physical war because of the time in history we live in. With the unrighteous madness of terrorism inflicted upon the innocent in our time, the inspiring words of Krishna may be taken out of context; however, I refuse to shy away from this speech because it is intended for good and can help one get closer to God. In our age, Muslim radicals have decided to terrorize the world by declaring a holy war in the name of God. They have used the term "jihad" to justify their actions. The Islamic term jihad means "struggle" and is a religious duty for Muslims. There are two forms of jihad in the Muslim faith. One refers to an internal struggle to live a moral and virtuous life and is called the greater jihad. The other refers to an external struggle to fight a holy war against the enemies of Islam and is called the lesser jihad. I pray that we all chose to fight the greater jihad within to live a moral and virtuous life and apply Krishna's advice to Arjuna to our personal lives and forget the lesser jihad of Muslim radicals who have dishonored God.

What I found most compelling in Hindu theology is the relationship between Atman and Brahman. Atman is the soul within a person, the innermost reality of a person and Brahman is the soul of the universe, the supreme infinite reality of the universe. Most compelling is the belief that Atman and Brahman are of the same essence, the same substance. Man's goal is to unite his soul with the soul of the universe. This can only be done if man can free himself from the bondage of worldly attachments and actions. Once freed, Atman becomes one with Brahman. The *Bhagavad-Gita* and the *Upanishads* teach the principles that will help one to free Atman into Brahman. The *Upanishads* - known for being the eternal wisdom of the Hindu mystics - is the most comprehensive text of theology behind this goal. It is the oldest scripture that I studied, but it remains fresh.

Taoism

Taoism is an ancient Chinese philosophy that became one of the great world religions. Its principal text is the *Tao Te Ching*. Probably a compilation of wisdom and insight from many sages, the *Tao Te Ching* began to take shape as far back as the seventh century BC, but most likely did not reach its final form until the mid-third century BC. However, tradition ascribes the authorship of the text to Lao Tzu, a seemingly legendary figure who is said to have been a contemporary of Confucius during the early sixth century BC.

With 81 short poem-like chapters, the text is primarily concerned with the Tao and Te. Taoism adopted its name from the Tao, which translates into English as "Way," as in the way the universe operates. It is the natural rhythm of the universe, the absolute reality of the universe. From before the beginning of time, it is the mysterious source of

Heaven and earth and the fountain of life for all life in the universe. The Tao is ethereal, yet substantial. It is invisible and vague, yet it has form and essence. It is unknowable, yet pervasive and trying to understand it can be difficult, but not hopeless.

In English, Te translates into "Virtue," as in the virtue characteristic of one who abides by the Tao. Te is the manifestation or power of the Tao in one who acts in accordance with the Tao. The underlying characteristic of Te is "wu-wei," which literally means "non-action," in essence, not to strive, like water, which does not contend. A person who is cautious, hesitant, polite, yielding, blank, open, and mixes freely (Addiss 15) is one who practices "wu-wei" and is called a sage. Like the Tao, Te is unfamiliar to many, if not most, and is difficult to comprehend and just as difficult to practice. The sage practices wu-wei and all things in the universe settle themselves and return to their natural state; harmony returns to the natural rhythm of the universe and all is restored, as it was meant to be. Wu-wei is not a form of apathy or recklessness. It means to take no unnatural action and to be one with the universe, with the Tao, which is "solitary and silent" (Addiss, 25). Understanding this, the world "moves without danger in safety and peace." (Addiss, 35). Everyone who reads the *Tao Te Ching* is encouraged to follow the example of the sage who is praiseworthy as benefactor to universe.

Ching means "classic work," so the *Tao Te Ching* neatly, yet roughly translates into "The Classic work of the Way and its Virtue."

Because of the great difficulty in translating Chinese into English, there are more than 100 translations of the *Tao Te Ching* in English. I first scrutinized the translation that I was introduced to at the university. Then, after extensive research, I scrutinized two additional translations that were popular and critically well received. Initially, I read each one like a novel from one chapter to the next, but when compelled, I returned to chapters that stuck with me. For years, I returned to the texts and I estimate I read the *Tao Te Ching* with earnest resolve at least twenty times. The *Tao Te Ching* was the most elusive, yet enlightening text I was reading at the time and it left a deep impression in my mind. I felt like I was unlocking the secrets of the eternal and I think that is the intention of the text. It is esoteric in nature and I believe few have delved into or have even been introduced to the profound depths of its wisdom. In addition to the *Tao Te Ching*, I read the *Chuang Tzu*, which is made up of brief stories and anecdotes, a delightful read and an important text in Taoism. However, no text, Taoist or otherwise, was as captivating as the *Tao Te Ching*. Its sublime beauty is exemplified in chapter 67, a favorite of mine. Though God the Father does not exist in Taoism, chapter 67 reminds me of a Christian sermon:

Everyone under heaven calls my Tao great,
And unlike anything else.

It is great only because
It is unlike anything else.
If it were like anything else
It would stretch and become thin.

I have three treasures
To maintain and conserve:
The first is compassion.
The second is frugality.
The third is not presuming
To be first under heaven.

Compassion leads to courage.
Frugality allows generosity.
Not presuming to be first
Creates a lasting instrument.

Nowadays
People reject compassion
But want to be brave,
Reject frugality
But want to be generous,
Reject humility
And want to come first.

This is death.

Compassion:
Attack with it and win.
Defend with it and stand firm.

Heaven aids and protects
Through compassion.

- *Tao Te Ching*, 67
(Translation S. Addiss and S. Lombardo)

Buddhism

Over four hundred years before Christ in South Asia by the Himalayas, a child was born named Siddhartha from the Sakya tribe, a prince of the Gautama clan, who would grow up to be known as the Buddha, meaning the "enlightened one" or "awakened one." When I first started studying the great world religions, I was quickly drawn to the story and teachings of the Buddha. I think what I found so appealing was his venerable goal to rid suffering from life. When the Buddha discovered the Four Noble Truths, he attained Enlightenment/Buddhahood/Nirvana. He taught these to his followers and if they were able to fully grasp them and experience them, they too would attain Enlightenment/Buddhahood/Nirvana and as a result, freedom from suffering. The Four Noble Truths are:

One, suffering is a part of existence: "Birth is suffering, aging is suffering, sickness is suffering, death is suffering: likewise, sorrow and grief, woe, lamentation and despair. To be conjoined with things which we dislike, to be separated from things which we like - that also is suffering. Not to get what one wants - that also is suffering. In a word, this body, this five-fold mass which is based on grasping - that is suffering."

Two, craving causes suffering: "It is that craving that leads back to birth, along with the lure and the lust that lingers longingly now here, now there: namely, the craving for sensual pleasure, the craving to be born again, the craving for existence to end."

Three, freedom from suffering is attained by letting go of craving: "It is the utter passionless cessation of, the giving up, the forsaking, the release from, the absence of longing for this craving."

Four, the way that leads to freedom from suffering is the Noble Eightfold Path's Middle Way: "Right views, right aim, right speech, right action, right living, right effort, right mindfulness, right concentration… This is that Middle Way which giveth vision, which

giveth knowledge, which causeth calm,
special knowledge, enlightenment, Nirvana."
The Middle Way is midway between
indulgent desire and extreme asceticism.

I appreciate Buddhism because it makes
sense. The Four Noble Truths constitute a sound
argument. As I studied them, I understood them,
intellectually. And, when I applied them to my life,
my experience affirmed their value. It takes a
lifetime, some Buddhists believe more than one
lifetime, to reach the
Enlightenment/Buddhahood/Nirvana of the Buddha.
Monks devote their lives to the teachings of the
Buddha and some never reach complete freedom
from suffering, the state of
Enlightenment/Buddhahood/Nirvana. I was no monk
and I know I was no further along the path to
Enlightenment/Buddhahood/Nirvana than they, but
during my earnest, humble quest, I believe I got a
taste of that sublime state and it was beautiful.

I was first exposed to the Four Noble Truths at
the university. Although, the class did not assign any
Buddhist scripture for study, we learned from lectures
and secondary readings. During my quest for wisdom
and truth and to better understand Buddhism, I found
a good book that included portions of authentic
Buddhist scripture. Of prime importance is "The
First Sermon." This was when the Buddha
expounded the Four Noble Truths for the first time to

five monks. This moment marked the Setting in Motion the Wheel of Dharma, which refers to the unceasing advancement of the Buddha's message taught by the faithful until the end of time. Through the book and further investigation, I discovered three important and influential sacred Buddhist texts: the *Dhammapada*, the *Lotus Sutra* and *The Way of the Bodhisattva*. The *Dhammapada* is an essential text in Theravada Buddhism. It reflects the essence of the Buddha's teachings. It is poetry and meditation. Reading it was rejuvenating like a cool breeze or a breath of fresh air or a tall glass of fresh water. Most uplifting is the teaching:

> Better than the sole rulership over the world,
> Better than going to heaven,
> Better than lordship over all the worlds,
> Is the fruition of the streamwinner's path.

> - *The Dhammapada*, 13.12
> (Translation A. Maitreya)

During my journey, with the *Bhagavad-Gita* or the *Dhammapada* in my pocket and reading daily during my travels, I felt like the streamwinner who is coming into his own.

While the *Dhammapada* is intimate as if the Buddha were speaking directly to you and guiding you, the *Lotus Sutra* relates the Buddha's teachings on a cosmic scale. It is a fundamental text in

Mahayana Buddhism. With poetic parables and speeches, it depicts multiple immortal spiritual Buddhas who are a part of an eternal massive spiritual universe. It illustrates the Buddhas' relationships with the universe and the role the individual plays in the universe with the Buddhas as his Light. Of great importance in the *Lotus Sutra* is the Bodhisattva who is "a being destined for Enlightenment/Buddhahood/Nirvana."

The clearest description of the Bodhisattva is in eighth century Indian Buddhist scholar Shantideva's *The Way of the Bodhisattva*. The Bodhisattva heroically postpones Enlightenment/Buddhahood/Nirvana out of great compassion for others in order to help others toward Enlightenment/Buddhahood/Nirvana. He vows to reach Enlightenment/Buddhahood/Nirvana for the benefit of all conscience living beings. In Mahayana Buddhism, everyone is encouraged to become a Bodhisattva. As I read *The Way of the Bodhisattva*, I did not want to put it down and when I was not reading it, I could barely wait to read it, again. It excited me to believe that I, too, could be a Bodhisattva and help save the world.

The *Dhammapada*, the *Lotus Sutra* and *The Way of the Bodhisattva* are very different, but all adhere to the teaching of the Four Noble Truths.

Human Inquiry
in Comparison to

God Attributed

Religions that come from human inquiry and religions that are God attributed have striking similarities and differences. When I decided to examine the great world religions, I had an innate belief that they have similarities because we are all human beings all living on the same planet. Compassion, wellbeing and eternal wisdom are cornerstones of each of the great world religions. As Plato recognized, we all inherently seek the Good. However, the great difference between the religions that come from human inquiry and the religions that are God attributed is belief in the One Almighty God. The religions of human inquiry (Hinduism, Taoism and Buddhism) do not teach that there is One Almighty God; while, the religions that are God attributed (Judaism, Christianity and Islam) do teach that there is One Almighty God.

Judaism

In my search for wisdom, truth and God, I was eager to examine the Jewish religion. Its value was obvious to me: it was the religion of my Lord - Jesus the Christ. As a Christian, I was familiar with Judaism and the monumental and grand stories in the Pentateuch (the first five books of the Old Testament), known in Judaism as the Torah. But, it was not until I inquired about Truth and the meaning of life that I decided I had to read the Jewish Scriptures for myself. I understood that the Old Testament in the Christian Bible was the Jewish Testament, but I was also aware that Jews do not study the Old Testament in the Christian Bible. I was vaguely aware that Jews study and worship from their own text. After some research, I discovered the Hebrew-English Tanakh from the Jewish Publication Society. To the average Christian, the only noticeable difference between the Old Testament in the Christian Bible and the Jewish Tanakh is that the Christian Bible's pages are ordered from left to right while the Tanakh is ordered from right to left. But, after scrutinizing the texts, I learned that there are subtle differences. So, I studied from the Tanakh because I wanted to study what Jews study. I focused on the book of Genesis and the book of Proverbs.

I studied the book of Genesis because I wanted to learn about the great stories and figures that are fundamental to all three monotheistic religions - the lessons to be learned from God's glory as Creator, from Adam and Eve's fall from grace, from the tragedy of Cain and Abel, from the righteous Noah and the great flood, from the megalomania of the Tower of Babel, from the lives and devotion of Patriarchs Abraham, Isaac and Jacob, and from the rise of Joseph. Each of these narratives is so important to the three monotheistic religions that I knew I had to learn them if I earnestly wanted to understand God and the wisdom and truth that I believed are inherent in each of the great world religions. The book of Proverbs, was of supreme value for my mission to find wisdom, truth and God. As I studied the great world religions' sacred scriptures, I found Proverbs to be the most accessible. It was clear and direct and I believed what it taught. It was practical. It was exactly what my mind was looking for. It taught me,

13 Happy is the man who finds wisdom,
The man who attains understanding.
14 Her [Wisdom's] value in trade is better than silver,
Her yield, greater than gold.
15 She is more precious than rubies;
All of your goods cannot equal her.

- Proverbs 3:13-15
(JPS Tanakh - Hebrew Bible/Old Testament)

Proverbs is a part of the wisdom literature found in the Jewish Scriptures. It was intended as instruction for, primarily, young men on their way to adulthood. At the time, I was a young man on my way to adulthood and I felt that Proverbs was made for me. I read Proverbs with joy and I applied its lessons to my life right away, but it would take me years to fully understand its teachings and utilize its value.

Islam

Islam's sacred scripture is the Qur'an. Like the Jewish Tanakh, the Qur'an's pages are ordered from right to left instead of left to right. When I first examined the Qur'an, I was surprised how important and integrated the Jewish and Christian Scriptures are to it; however, the style of writing is very different. There is constant repetition in the themed chapters. Its structure is poetic and Allah (God) is constantly addressed within the writing style. We are taught that Allah is Beneficent, Merciful, the Lord of Worlds, Master of the Day of Judgment, Creator, Protector, Lord of Mighty Grace, Forgiving, Ample Giving, Knowing, Hearing, Mighty, Wise, Affectionate, Grateful and is described in many other ways. Ultimately, we are taught that Allah is Powerful and that we must submit to Him and be obedient to Him.

Muslims believe that the Qur'an is Allah's final revelation to humankind and that Muhammad was chosen by Allah to deliver that revelation. In the Qur'an, believers and unbelievers of the revelation are strictly divided from another, but as a young Christian who was looking for answers, I focused not on the divide, but on the truths I saw in the Qur'an.

Islam is unmistakably linked to the previous monotheistic religions: Judaism and Christianity. I was most surprised to see Jesus and Mother Mary in the Qur'an. Jesus is referred to as Messiah and

Mother Mary as Virgin. For example, in chapter 3 of the Qur'an, we are told,

45. When the angles said: O Marium [Mary], surely Allah [God] gives you good news with a Word from Him (of one) whose name is Messiah, Isa [Jesus] son of Marium, worthy of regard in this world and the hereafter and of those who are made near (to Allah).

46. And he shall speak to the people when in the cradle and when of old age, and (he shall be) one of the good ones.

47. She said: My Lord! when shall there be a son (born) to me, and man has not touched me? He said: Even so, Allah creates what He pleases; when He has decreed a matter, He only says to it, Be, and it is.

48. And He will teach him the Book and the wisdom and the Taurat [Torah] and the Injeel [Gospel].

49. And (make him) an apostle to the children of Israel: That I have come to you with a sign from your Lord, that I determine for you out of dust like the form of a bird, then I breathe into it and it becomes a bird with

Allah's permission and I heal the blind and the leprous, and bring the dead to life with Allah's permission and I inform you of what you should eat and what you should store in your houses; most surely there is a sign in this for you, if you are believers.

50. And a verifier of that which is before me of the Taurat, and that I may allow you part of that which has been forbidden you, and I have come to you with a sign from your Lord, therefore be careful of (your duty to) Allah and obey me.

51. Surely Allah is my Lord and your Lord, therefore serve Him; this is the right path.

- Qur'an, Surah III, 45-51
(Translation M. H. Shakir)

I never finished reading the Qur'an - there is so much - but I read approximately 65 percent of it.

Christianity

I was born a Christian. My roots are firmly secured in the Christian religion, which is why I decided to study it last in order to give proper attention to the other great world religions and learn what they had to teach. I never lost sight of Jesus.

He was always with me, but he was not in the forefront of my thoughts as I investigated the other religions. When I finally decided to examine my Christian religion, I concentrated on the four Gospels. Eventually, my enthusiasm grew and I searched for any and all types of literature to satisfy my hunger for knowledge of Jesus the Christ.

I believe in God Almighty. And, I believe that Christianity is the means to God Almighty. When I have a question, I first refer to the Bible, particularly the New Testament. Jesus's words are never far from my heart and mind. There is no doubt that Jesus walked the earth, that he existed historically, but some people doubt that he is the Christ.

I knew that Jesus was the Christ - God's Anointed One - when I discovered the Old Testament prophecy of God's Suffering Servant. It depicts Jesus's suffering and death and his mission and scope - even though it was written over 500 years before he arrived. It reads:

> [Isaiah 52]
> 13 Behold, my servant shall prosper,
>   he shall be exalted and lifted up,
>   and shall be very high.
> 14 As many were astonished at him[b]—
>   his appearance was so marred, beyond
> human semblance,

and his form beyond that of the sons of
men—
15 so shall he startle[c] many nations;

kings shall shut their mouths because of
him;
for that which has not been told them they
shall see,

and that which they have not heard they
shall understand.

[Isaiah 53]
Who has believed what we have heard?

And to whom has the arm of the Lord been
revealed?
2 For he grew up before him like a young
plant,

and like a root out of dry ground;
he had no form or comeliness that we should
look at him,

and no beauty that we should desire him.
3 He was despised and rejected[a] by men;

a man of sorrows,[b] and acquainted with
grief;[c]
and as one from whom men hide their faces

he was despised, and we esteemed him not.
4 Surely he has borne our griefs[d]

and carried our sorrows;[e]
yet we esteemed him stricken,

smitten by God, and afflicted.
5 But he was wounded for our transgressions,

he was bruised for our iniquities;
upon him was the chastisement that made us whole,
    and with his stripes we are healed.
6 All we like sheep have gone astray;
    we have turned every one to his own way;
and the Lord has laid on him
    the iniquity of us all.
7 He was oppressed, and he was afflicted,
    yet he opened not his mouth;
like a lamb that is led to the slaughter,
    and like a sheep that before its shearers is dumb,
    so he opened not his mouth.
8 By oppression and judgment he was taken away;
    and as for his generation, who considered
that he was cut off out of the land of the living,
    stricken for the transgression of my people?
9 And they made his grave with the wicked
    and with a rich man in his death,
although he had done no violence,
    and there was no deceit in his mouth.
10 Yet it was the will of the Lord to bruise him;
    he has put him to grief;[f]
when he makes himself[g] an offering for sin,
    he shall see his offspring, he shall prolong his days;

the will of the Lord shall prosper in his hand;
11   he shall see the fruit of the travail of his soul and be satisfied;
by his knowledge shall the righteous one, my servant,
   make many to be accounted righteous;
   and he shall bear their iniquities.
12 Therefore I will divide him a portion with the great,
   and he shall divide the spoil with the strong;
because he poured out his soul to death,
   and was numbered with the transgressors;
yet he bore the sin of many,
   and made intercession for the transgressors.

- Isaiah 52:13-53:12
(RSV Bible)

When I first read this, my heart broke open and a flood of tears poured out. I could barely read it once, but when I did, I needed to read it again and again. Truly, Jesus is the Christ. He fulfills the Old Testament promise. He replaces Israel as the means of Salvation. He is God's Suffering Servant.

Jews and Muslims overlook the truth that Jesus is the Christ and the Son of God because of the hardness of their hearts denying His Love and Passion. Jesus explains to us that,

40 "He who receives you receives me, and he who receives me receives him who sent me. 41 He who receives a prophet because he is a prophet shall receive a prophet's reward, and he who receives a righteous man because he is a righteous man shall receive a righteous man's reward. 42 And whoever gives to one of these little ones even a cup of cold water because he is a disciple, truly, I say to you, he shall not lose his reward."

- Matthew 10:40-42
(RSV Bible)

But, I say to you that Jesus is not just a righteous man and he is more than a prophet; he is the Son of God and he who receives the Son of God because he is the Son of God shall receive the Son's reward. All who believe in Jesus and live according to his teachings will be given the right to enter Paradise because they acknowledge him as the Way, the Truth and the Life. He is the Door of the Sheepfold and all who enter through him will enter Paradise.

As I accrued all this information about the great world religions, connections between them became apparent and the world became a smaller place. I was growing spiritually and confidently. I believed that the religions that I was learning were making me wiser. As I was growing up, I desired physical strength, but now, I sought mental and spiritual strength. My priorities had changed and I devoted myself to the teachings of God seeking the fruits of my spiritual labor.

I was inspired by my heroes and I would cry when I heard about their greatness. There was kinship between me and my heroes in the world - revolutionaries, athletes, artists, musicians - because I, too, wanted to be great and at times, I saw their greatness in me. I wanted to be like these men - men like Mohandas Gandhi, the Mahatma, the Great Soul. He carried the Indian nation to freedom from the British Empire - one of the most powerful empires in recent history - without a sword. His wisdom paralleled that of King Solomon. It was said that during the peak of Hindu and Muslim strife in India, a Hindu anarchist confessed to Gandhi that he killed a Muslim child by smashing the child's head against a wall because the Muslims killed his son. Gandhi told the man that he knew a way out of Hell. He told the man, a Hindu, to find a Muslim boy, his enemy's son, whose parents had been killed in the strife and to raise and nurture the boy as his own, only to be sure that he, a Hindu, raise the boy to be a Muslim, the faith of this enemy. The brilliant Albert Einstein was quoted saying, "Generations to come will scarce believe that such a one as this ever in flesh and blood walked upon this Earth." All my heroes had a passion for life and each one touched my soul. But, no one meant more to me than my Lord Jesus the Christ who taught me about God and the true love between God and man and love between neighbors.

My soul was filled with joy because I knew I was on the right path. I was absorbing the teachings that I learned from the great world religions and the seed of inspiration was budding. I needed to express my internal religious growth and maturity externally. The first stage was keeping a journal, but before formulating my own ideas and interpretations, I cataloged what I learned. And, in my bedroom with my books as I was coming to know God, I posted on my walls many of the wonderful teachings I learned and retained. I surrounded myself with those beautiful and powerful sayings that meant the most to me. They were becoming a part of me and I loved it. However, I was torn between the realities of Heaven and earth and all the euphoric beauty of heavenly wisdom that I learned would conflict with a world that was concerned with its own self interests.

There is a triumph of truth's consistency among the great world religions that there is something with us that is greater than the universe, yet intimately connected to oneself. As a Christian, I believe this is God and that He is our Father, but the other great world religions are not wrong when they describe His Power. All the great world religions aim to unite us with God. Union with God is the reason for living and the final goal. However, it is only possible through Jesus the Christ who is the Way to God the Father.

Every day, I try to serve God. There are many ways to serve Him. We are each gifted with different strengths. The Christian saints are proof of this. No two saints are the same. Each is a person with his or her own identity, but each one serves God. I read and write and try to help those in need. Your path may be different. I tell you to take life seriously and get to know yourself. Find your passion and become all you can be. Take that passion and direct it toward God. Make God your first priority and everything else will work itself out. As long as God's love is in you and it remains in you, you will not go wrong.

DANTE'S *DIVINE COMEDY*

JAMES THOMAS ANGELIDIS

The following is my graduate school paper about the allegorical nature of Dante's Divine Comedy - a trilogy about Hell, Purgatory and Heaven.

Most people are familiar with Dante's *Inferno* - a fascinating book with vivid imagery about one man's journey through Hell. The mood is dark because Hell is dark, but it is only the beginning of the protagonist's journey. Dante wrote two other books called *Purgatorio* and *Paradiso* and they are about the protagonist's journey through Purgatory and Heaven. Together, the three books complete a set that is known as the *Divine Comedy*. The meaning of the word "comedy" in the title is not the same as the word comedy used in common daily dialogue that refers to amusement and humor. Comedy from the

Divine Comedy refers to a literary genre where the story has a happy ending - unlike a tragedy that ends badly. This is true of Dante's work because at the end, the protagonist encounters God. Dante titled the work, simply, *Comedy*. The word divine was added by a fellow Italian poet, but was not incorporated into the title until over 200 years after Dante wrote the work.

I studied the *Divine Comedy* as a theology student in graduate school. For one semester, along with my other classes, I worked independently with my professor and wrote a 30 page paper on the set. Below is the product of a fascinating and enlightening four months. The *Divine Comedy* can be read on a literal level and on an allegorical level. Dante wrote the work to turn people away from sin and seek God. He wants to wake people up before it is too late and their eternal fates are finalized. The work is a piece of art - an epic poem that stirs the imagination. The protagonist is Dante - a shadow of the author himself - who journeys through Hell, Purgatory and Heaven. However, below the surface are hidden truths and lessons to be learned. The protagonist Dante represents the whole of humankind in the world and his journey is an allegory for humankind's journey toward God. In my paper, I focused on Dante's three guides. They represent the three lights in the world that help people see - with the brightest light at highest height that we can reach. The protagonist Dante sees what he sees because of the guides. They show him. Through them, he sees. These guides allegorically represent the light of Reason, the light of Faith and the light of Glory. They are the means to union with God. Dante is an artist at the highest level because through his art he is able to teach.

Introduction

Dante Alighieri was born in 1265 and died in 1321. He is one of Italy's greatest poets and his *Divine Comedy* is considered a "masterpiece of world literature"[1] and the "greatest Christian poem."[2] The narrative of the *Divine Comedy* describes Dante's journey through the deepest depths of Hell, up Mount Purgatory and then to Heaven where God dwells. This narrative is an allegory for every individual in this world, for his journey and often times, his struggle to find peace in this world with the hope of Salvation. Allegory abounds in the *Divine Comedy* and recognizing it is essential to understanding the many meanings in the text. Like all allegories, it tells a story in which "characters and events stand for abstract ideas, principles, or forces, so that the literal sense has or suggests a parallel, deeper symbolic sense."[3] Ultimately, the protagonist Dante in the

---

[1] Christopher Ryan, "Dante Alighieri," in *The Oxford Companion to Christian Thought,* ed. Adrian Hastings, (Oxford: Oxford University Press, 2000), 149.

[2] *Encyclopedia Britannica*, "Dante," 1970.

[3] *American Heritage Dictionary*, "Allegory," 1996.

Divine Comedy is "the image of every Christian sinner and his pilgrimage is that which every soul must take."[4] In *Journey to Beatrice*, Singleton explains that the story has,

> a meaning for all to see who may happen to find themselves in a dark and bitter wood of sin, who by God's grace may be privileged to turn, in a dawning light, toward a summit where justice and grace and reunion with God may be attained, and who from that first summit may be further privileged to rise to the higher peak of perfected grace and of final beatitude, *while still in this life.*[5]

Yes - "*while still in this life.*" Dante's story is for the living not the dead. With the help of Singleton and other scholars, I will investigate the allegorical nature of Dante's *Divine Comedy*. Dante's journey is not merely a mesmerizing story of a character's journey through the afterlife among the souls of the departed. More importantly, the journey is what medieval theologians called *Itinerarium Mentis Ad Deum* - the journey of the mind and heart, the will and intellect to God. In this work, I will investigate

---

[4] Dorothy Sayers, Introduction, *The Divine Comedy I: Hell,* by Dante Alighieri. ed. and trans. with notes, by Dorothy L. Sayers. (London: Penguin Books, 1949), 67.
[5] Charles S. Singleton, *Journey to Beatrice* (Baltimore: The John's Hopkins University Press, 1977), 7.

the three lights that lead Dante to the unmediated vision of God granted through the gift of what is called the Beatific Vision. Those three lights are personified by his three guides: Virgil as an allegory for the light of Reason, Beatrice as an allegory for the light of Faith and Saint Bernard as an allegory for the light of Glory.

Virgil as an Allegory for the Light of Reason

Virgil represents the light of Reason - the most natural light in man in his journey to God. In comparison to the light of Glory, which is exemplified by Saint Bernard, and the light of Faith, which is exemplified by Beatrice, the light of Reason is the least bright light in man's journey to God.

Historically, Virgil is considered Rome's greatest poet. He was born near Mantua and lived from 70 BC to 19 BC. He is the celebrated author of the *Aeneid*, a national epic and considered one of the greatest pieces of literature in world history. It tells of the origin and destiny of the Roman Empire and its role as leader in the civilized world. The main character is Aeneas who is a "paragon of Roman virtues - familial devotion, loyalty to the state, and piety."[6]

In the *Divine Comedy*, Dante uses Virgil to show that man has the ability to improve himself and

---

[6] *Concise Columbia Encyclopedia*, "Virgil," 1994.

ascend to God through Reason. However, it is important to understand that Reason does not make man perfect. Reason has limits. Virgil's strengths and weaknesses symbolize the strengths and weakness of Reason. As Glazov explains, "Virgil emerges in the poem as the kind of light which 'philosophers' had, who did not have the second and higher light of faith and of sanctifying grace - a fact already apparent in Virgil's confessed limits as guide."[7] Singleton explains,

> Such a light would remain with man even after Adam's sin and after the privation of sanctifying grace which resulted from that sin. Thus it is the light by which the "philosophers" saw whatever truths they did see, since they were deprived of the light of faith or of revelation or of sanctifying grace, and could move in the way of intellect only by the natural light of reason. That light was their only guide *in via*. Plato, therefore, and Aristotle, and all the other virtuous pagans "who did not sin" had this light, natural to man, and no other light of intellect than this. Because this is so, these "philosophers" shall never enjoy that higher light which is Beatrice

---

[7] Gregory Glazov, "The Spiritual Journey in the Divine Comedy Part II: The Three Lights." A Microsoft Office PowerPoint presentation. South Orange, New Jersey. 18 January 2011. Slide 10.

and which is the light given to the "saints" *in via*; nor of course shall they ever see by that yet higher light of glory which is man's last beatitude. What was denied them in this life is denied them in eternity. Every reader knows the pathos that attaches to the figure of Virgil because of this hard truth.[8]

Singleton is a celebrated scholar. Hatzfeld's calls *Journey to Beatrice* a "most splendid Dante interpretation" and Singleton "one of the great explicators of the medieval mind and art in our time."[9] Singleton points out that Dante did not invent the analogy of three lights; rather, it was a notion he adopted from the theology of his day. Any reader of the *Divine Comedy* who is introduced to Saint Thomas Aquinas's *In Isaiam Prophetam* will clearly see the parallels between the theologies in the two works, both of which seem to have adopted it from a common theological tradition. Though perhaps not obvious today, Dante seems to have taken the familiar theology of his day to create the allegorical *Divine Comedy*.

The author Dante chose Virgil to be the protagonist Dante's guide through two-thirds of his journey in the afterlife - through Hell and up to the

---

[8] Singleton, *Journey to Beatrice*, 33.

[9] Helmut Hatzfeld, review of *Journey to Beatrice*, by Charles S. Singleton, *Modern Language Journal*, vol. 43, no. 7 (Nov. 1959): 354-55.

final level of Mount Purgatory. This is significant because Dante (the author) is a Christian and is the author of the *Divine Comedy*, the "greatest Christian poem,"[10] and Virgil is a pagan. For the majority of this most Christian of Christian works, the protagonist Dante follows Virgil, a pagan, and calls him "master" and "lord." How can this be? How can a Christian follow a pagan and call him master and lord when there is one Master and Lord - Jesus Christ. Very telling is what the protagonist Dante says at the beginning of *Inferno* when he is in the Dark Wood after he is confronted by the three beasts who prevent him from climbing up the Mountain. Lost in the Dark Wood, Dante is met by Virgil. Stunned, he says:

> "Canst thou be Virgil? thou that fount of splendour
> Whence poured to wide a stream of lordly speech?"
> Said I, and bowed my awe-struck head in wonder;
> "O honour and light of poets all and each,
> Now let my great love stead me - the bent brow
> And long hours pondering all thy book can teach!
> Thou art my master, and my author thou,
> From thee alone I learned the in strain,

---

[10] *Encyclopedia Britannica*, "Dante," 1970.

The noble style, that does me honour now
(*Inferno,* 1.79-87).[11]

For Dante, "Virgil wasn't a normal man… [He] was a
Roman poet, exalted and legitimized by the staying
power of more than 13 centuries."[12] Hollander
explains that in the poem, "Dante could not do
without him [Virgil]. Virgil is the guide in Dante's
poem because he served in that role in Dante's life."[13]

Like most cultured men, Dante believed that
art, particularly poetry, had the power to persuade and
therefore persuade his fellow man to seek Salvation.
"A poet above all, he felt that only in poetry, which
goes beyond the closed abstractions of a scientific
treatise, would he be able to express fully his
dream… of a spiritual and civil renewal of the whole
of humanity."[14] More than Plato or Aristotle, Dante
adored Virgil because Virgil was what Dante aspired
to be like - a Roman poet, exalted and legitimized by
a staying power that would last centuries. Virgil was
proud to be an Italian. He believed in the glory of
Rome. As evident in the *Aeneid,* Roman culture
valued the team over the individual; unlike the

---

[11] Dante Alighieri, *The Divine Comedy I: Hell*, ed. and
trans. with notes, by Dorothy L. Sayers (London: Penguin
Books, 1949), 73.

[12] "Virgil's Role in the Divine Comedy." *Dante and
Virgil: A Study of Poetry, Language and History.* (January 18,
2011). http://users.rcn.com/antos/dante/divine_com.html

[13] Robert Hollander, *Dante: A Life in Works* (New
Haven: Yale University Press, 2001), 116.

Greeks, who held more esteem for the individual, as is evident in the journeys of one man in the *Odyssey*. I believe Dante saw truth in the Roman perspective and in his theology, he showed that, unlike the solitude of Hell, Heaven is a place of community.

Though Dante revered the author Virgil, he did not fashion the character Virgil as an ideal to be emulated. He fashioned Virgil flawed to show the limitations and weakness of Reason. For example, at the start of Canto IX, when Dante and Virgil wait for Divine assistance to enter the City of Dis, Dante and Virgil look at each other and notice the fear in the other:

> Seeing my face, and what a coward colour
> It turned when he came back, my guide was quick
> To put away his own unwonted pallor."

Dante explains that "So black the air was, and the fog so thick" to symbolize the ominous situation. Filled with anxiety awaiting for Divine assistance, Virgil cries out, "But oh! how long his coming seems to be!" (*Inferno* 9.1-9).[15] Virgil's anxiety at this moment symbolizes the weakness of Reason when reason is confronted with fear. Reason has the potential to crumble when things are uncertain; but, with the Light of Glory - Faith, Hope and Love - there

---

[14] *Encyclopedia Britannica*, "Dante," 1970.
[15] Dante Alighieri, *The Divine Comedy I: Hell*, 123.

is no fear.

Another example depicting Virgil's flawed nature is in Canto XII when Virgil taunts the Minotaur. Here, Virgil shouts,

> "… How now, hellion!
> Thinkst thou the Duke of Athens comes anew,
> That slew they in the upper world? Begone,
> Monster! not guided by thy sister's clue
> Has this man come; only to see and know
> Your punishments, he threads the circle through."
> Then as a bull pierced by the mortal blow
> Breaks loose, and cannot go straight, but reels in the ring
> Plunging wildly and staggering to and fro,
> I saw the Minotaur fall a-floundering,
> And my wary guide called: Run! run for the pass!
> Make good thy going now, while his rage has its fling"
> (*Inferno*, 12.16-27).[16]

Virgil shows no respect for his adversary and mocks him as "his rage has its fling." Reason can be cruel and unrelenting when left to its own devices. However, the Light of Glory brings peace, not anger.

An additional example is found in Canto XXI

---

[16] Dante Alighieri, *The Divine Comedy I: Hell*, 142-143.

when Virgil trusts the advice of Belzecue, the chief Demon, who directs Dante and Virgil to follow a path that he contests is safe. Later on in Canto XXIII, the Jovial Friar Catalano mocks Virgil because he listened to Belzecue who, as a demon, should never be trusted. Depicting Virgil's reaction to the news, Dante explains,

> My guide stood with bent head and downward look
> A while; then said: He gave us bad advice,
> Who spears the sinners yonder with his hook."
> And the Friar: "I heard the devil's iniquities
> Much canvassed at Bologna; among the rest
> 'Twas said, he was a liar and father of lies."
> My guide with raking steps strode off in haste,
> Troubled in his looks, and showing some small heat
> Of anger
> (*Inferno*, 23.139-147).[17]

This episode represents the insufficiency of Reason, which can fail without the light of Glory. It can be fooled. The representatives of evil know this and take advantage of Reason's weaknesses. The above examples represent the insufficiency of Reason working on its own without the light of Glory. As Ryan explains, "Supremely civilized though he may

---

[17] Dante Alighieri, *The Divine Comedy I: Hell*, 217.

be, Virgil is from the outset of the comedy a fatally flawed figure, his limitation serving to illustrate the plight of humankind when left to its own devices, without the benefit of Christ."[18]

Flawed, Virgil is, nonetheless, lovable. Sayers explains that "Virgil fills the first two books of the poem; and in making him so central and so lovable and in then rending him clean out of the story, Dante took a risk which only the very greatest of artists could venture or afford to take."[19] Dante was honest with himself and great artists are always true to themselves. He did not allow his affinity to Virgil overpower his plan to spread the Word as a Christian and prophet.

Virgil is Dante's guide through Hell and Purgatory and by better knowing Hell and Purgatory, we can better know Virgil and what he represents. In *Inferno*, Hell is made up of nine concentric circles descending below the earth. The levels and the departed represent the seven deadly sins with the deepest, most distant from God at the bottom - pride being the most severe sin. Satan is the most prideful - so in love with himself that he wanted to be like God and usurp God's power - and resides at the pit's bottom. In Dante's Hell, "surprisingly and revealingly, [there] contains very little of the … meditations on death that communicate a contempt

---

[18] Ryan, "Dante Alighieri," 150.
[19] Dorothy L. Sayers, *Further Papers on Dante* (London: Methuen and Co., 1957), 59.

for life."[20] Rather, it focuses on sin and Virgil's warnings to Dante that as you see the damned sinners, so, too, will you be if you follow their paths. Hell is an allegory for the severity of sins that eat away at one's soul. "It is the condition to which the soul reduces itself by a stubborn determination to evil, and in which it suffers the torment of its own perversions."[21] Dante's Hell illustrates the ills that hinder one's journey to God. Virtues bring the individual closer to God, while sins distance the individual from God. In the individual, at first, sins are venial and seem harmless, like eating too many sweets or fibbing. But, then, they can grow and become habits - like gluttony or cheating, which direct the intellect and will away from God. Venial sins can become a gateway to vices and can corrupt the individual and twist his understanding of truth. This regression is allegorized and illustrated by the tortured souls in the narrative of the *Inferno.* During his journey through Hell, Dante recognizes the wrathful Filippo Agenti and apprehends the truth about sin, curses it and is reborn spiritually. Dante shouts at Filippo, "Accursed spirit, do thou remain and rot! / I know thee, filthy as thou art - I know." Proud and pleased, Virgil lays his arms about Dante's neck and kisses him saying, "Indignant soul, Blessed

[20] Ricardo J. Quinones, "Inferno," in *The Dante Encyclopedia*, ed. Lansing, Richard (New York: Garland Publishing, Inc., 2000), 511.

[21] Sayers, Introduction, *The Divine Comedy I: Hell,* 68.

is the womb that bare thee!" (*Inferno* 8.37-45).[22]

In *Purgatorio*, Purgatory is a mountain with seven levels, each corresponding to one of the seven deadly sins. The higher one climbs and overcomes each sin, the closer one will be to God. On each level, the souls of the departed "are purged successively of the taint of the seven deadly sins, and so made fit to ascend into the presence of God in Paradise."[23] They purge their sins by practicing the opposite virtues. They make themselves fit to enter Paradise through good habits, a theology not far from the Aristotelian philosophy which contests that "we are what we repeatedly do. Excellence, therefore, is not an act, but a habit" (Will Durant, *The Story of Philosophy*, 76). The souls in Purgatory move with urgency to reach Heaven. Purgatory is about the passage from time to eternity, the overcoming of sin, repentance, redemption and the hope of attaining Salvation. Like the souls in Purgatory, man living in the world must liberate his intellect and will from the shackles of sin which prevent him from reaching God.

Virgil is Dante's guide up the mountain, but is incapable of entering earthly paradise. As the light of Reason, Virgil is insufficient to journey further to God. He has traveled as far as he could and is elated when he reaches the top of the mountain with Dante and tells Dante,

---

[22] Dante Alighieri, *The Divine Comedy I: Hell*, 117.
[23] Sayers, Introduction, *The Divine Comedy I: Hell,* 69.

See how the sun shines here upon thy head;
See the green sward, the flowers, the boscages
That from the soil's own virtue here are bred
While those fair eyes are coming, bright with bliss,
Whose tears sent me to thee, thou may'st prospect
At large, or sit at ease to view all this.
No word from me, no further sign expect;
Free, upright, whole, thy will henceforth lays down
Guidance that it were error to neglect,
Whence o'er thyself I mitre thee and crown
(*Purgatorio,* 27.133-142).[24]

Virgil cannot comprehend Dante's ultimate destination - the Beatific Vision of God Himself - and so he is overwhelmed with joy when he reaches his peak - the sight of earthly paradise. The Light of Reason can take us only so far and even at its highest, Reason cannot reach Faith's heights. So, protagonist Dante will see that which Virgil cannot by means of Faith, which is allegorized by Dante's next guide, Beatrice. Schnapp contests that,

Virgil's role was defined as transitional from

---

[24] Dante Alighieri, *The Divine Comedy II: Purgatory*, ed. and trans. with notes, by Dorothy L. Sayers. (London: Penguin Books, 1955), 285.

the outset. His task was to guide his charge to another guide. [His] mission is completed at the mountain's summit, where Dante-pilgrim's will is pronounced 'free, upright and whole.' Until this juncture Virgil's guidance had been indispensable to the pilgrim's progress. Now it has reached its term, and Virgil can discern no further."[25]

Very interesting and insightful is Sayers's perspective on the relationship between Dante and Virgil in Purgatory. In one of my favorite observations, Sayers explains,

> Into this realm [Purgatory], Virgil could not go without Dante; he is still his companion but no longer in the strict sense his guide. Yet Dante needs him, since in the story, Virgil is his "contact" in the spirit-world, and lends him eyes to see those "secret things" which are hidden from mortal view.[26]

Virgil cannot go without Dante because Virgil does not have access to the realm of Purgatory by himself. Virgil resides in Limbo, the first circle of hell, where

---

[25] Jeffrey T. Schnapp, "Purgatorio," in *The Dante Encyclopedia,* ed. Richard Lansing (New York: Garland Publishing, Inc., 2000), 726.

[26] Dorothy L. Sayers, *Introductory Papers on Dante* (London: Methuen and Co., 1954), 108.

the unbaptized and virtuous pagans dwell. But, he is permitted to visit Purgatory because of Dante and Dante needs Virgil to see in the spirit-world. They need each other, which makes their bond stronger, which is why it is difficult to see Virgil go from the remainder of the narrative.

The author Dante honors and loves Virgil. However, Dante's destiny for Virgil is one in which he is trapped in Limbo forever, never to ascend to the heavens. As Sayers explains in *Further Papers on Dante*,

> The whole theme of the Comedy is that Virgil is fundamental, indispensable, and yet of himself inadequate. Man is inadequate. Natural Reason and Art, Natural Morality, Natural Religion, if without Grace, without Revelation, without Redemption, cannot at their best attain any higher state than Limbo.[27]

Pellegrini attests that Sayers "exhibits a keen sensitivity to the richness of meaning that attaches to Dante's Virgil, and all her Virgils do revolve about the central point of his exclusion from salvation."[28] Sayers attests that Reason is not enough for Salvation. She explains that "Virgil is the best of all that Man by

---

[27] Sayers, *Further Papers on Dante*, 60.
[28] Anthony L. Pellegrini, review of *Further Papers on Dante*, by Dorothy L. Sayers, *Speculum*, vol. 35, no. 1 (Jan. 1960): 143.

his own nature has and is; and it is not enough."[29] Crissman contests that Virgil "must have had a perfect will," which is "mastery of reason over the appetite."[30] And, still, he is inadequate to climb further.

Purgatory is a realm where philosophy cannot travel without theology. Without the help of theology, philosophy does not understand the degradation of sin. Philosophy recognizes the distinction between virtues and vices and can even persuade one to live a virtuous life. It has that potential - but it is unconvinced. Theology is convinced that a virtuous life is the only way to live because it brings one closer to God. Philosophy does not know God. If it did, it would be theology. Philosophy can be purified through theology and will reach its full potential by means of theology, but philosophy without theology lacks God's blessings. Until philosophy embraces theology, it remains in Limbo.

When Virgil and Dante reach earthly paradise, they meet Beatrice. However, she is mentioned during their journey heightening Dante's expectation to be reunited with her, his most loved. Reaching the second level of Mount Purgatory, Dante asks Virgil

---

[29] Sayers, *Further Papers on Dante*, 66.
[30] Charley Crissman, "The Tragedy of Virgil." (18 January 2011) http://www.gmalivuk.com/otherstuff/otherpeople/charley_Trage dyvirgil.html

about the efficacy of payer. With an interim answer, Virgil says,

> These are deep waters; rest not there - reject
> Conclusion, till she show it thee who is
> Set as a light 'twixt truth and intellect -
> I know not if thou understandest this:
> I mean Beatrice; on this mount's high crest
> Thou shalt behold her, smiling and in bliss
> (*Purgatorio*, 6.43-48).[31]

Between truth and intellect, Beatrice is the next light in the movement toward God.

Beatrice as an Allegory for the Light of Faith

The character of Beatrice in Dante's *Divine Comedy* personifies the light of Faith and only with Faith can Dante journey through Heaven. Once Virgil has fulfilled his duty as guide to Dante, Beatrice takes over and leads Dante to the Empyrean where God dwells. Both Virgil and Beatrice serve as guides to Dante, but they are very different and represent different disciplines and institutions. Glazov explains that Virgil represents the light of Reason, Philosophy, the State, the Secular; while, Beatrice represents the light of Faith, Theology, the

---

[31] Dante Alighieri, *The Divine Comedy II: Purgatory*, 111.

Church, the Religious.[32] Though they are different they do not conflict with one another. In fact, as Dante intimates, there is a courteous relationship between the two guides and therefore, the two Lights. At the beginning of the *Divine Comedy*, Beatrice humbles herself and entreats Virgil's assistance to guide her friend Dante on his journey:

> 'O courteous Mantuan soul, whose skill in song
> Keeps green on earth a fame that shall not end
> While motion rolls the turning spheres along!
> A friend of mine, who is not Fortune's friend,
> Is hard beset upon the shadowy coast;
> Terrors and snares his fearful steps attend,
> Driving him back; yea, and I fear almost
> I have risen too late to help - for I was told
> Such news of him in Heaven - he's too far
> lost.
> But thou - go thou! Lift up thy voice of gold;
> Try every needful means to find and reach
> And free him, that my heart may rest
> consoled.
> Beatrice am I, who thy good speed beseech;
> Love that first moved me from the blissful
> place

---

[32] Gregory Glazov, "The Spiritual Journey in the Divine Comedy, Final Part." A Microsoft Office PowerPoint presentation. South Orange, New Jersey. 18 January 2011. Slide 10.

Whither I'd fain return, now moves my speech (*Inferno*, 2.58-72).[33]

Beatrice knows she can rely on Virgil and that they must work together to lead Dante to the Beatific Vision of God. Their roles in the *Divine Comedy* are crystallized in verse form when Virgil tells Dante that,

> "So much as reason here distinguisheth
> I can unfold," said he; "thereafter, sound
> Beatrice's mind alone, for that needs faith"
> (Purgatorio, 18.46-48).[34]

Here, it is clear that Virgil represents the light of Reason and Beatrice the light of Faith. Unlike the light of Reason, the light of Faith is beyond human comprehension, yet it guides us nonetheless. Beyond the senses, Dante's journey with Beatrice is also beyond intelligence. Like Dante, we Christians seek the higher realm, which can only be reached by means of Faith. Singleton explains,

> ... for all the "sense" experience which is had in this high sphere where Beatrice guides, the poet has made it clear beyond any doubt that this journey with her is one "surpassing the

---

[33] Dante Alighieri, *The Divine Comedy I: Hell*, 79-80.
[34] Dante Alighieri, *The Divine Comedy II: Purgatory*, 206.

human intelligence." To pass from Virgil's guidance to that of Beatrice means, when measured on the familiar pattern, to pass from journey by the first of three lights to journey by the second.[35]

Dante's Beatrice in the *Divine Comedy* is an extension of the historical Beatrice - his true life-love - who he celebrates in his earlier work, *Vita Nuova*. The light of Faith is the second of the three theological lights that were recognized during the Middle Ages. Saint Thomas Aquinas in his *Contra Gentiles* explains that "man's knowledge of divine things is threefold." Saint Thomas explains that after Reason, Faith is when,

> the divine truth which surpasses the human intelligence comes down to us by revelation, yet not as shown to him [man] that he may see it, but as expressed in words so that he may hear it."[36]

Dante met Beatrice only twice, but he loved her from a distance and his love for her remained constant throughout his life and will last unto the ages in his writings. As he writes in the *Vita Nuova,* "I hope to compose concerning her what has never been

---

[35] Charles S. Singleton, *Journey to Beatrice* (Baltimore: The John's Hopkins University Press, 1977), 25.

[36] Cited by Singleton, *Journey to Beatrice*, 23.

written in rhyme of any woman." Most scholars believe that Beatrice is Beatrice Portinari from Florence, the daughter of Folco Portinari, a wealthy banker. Biographical information is limited, but it appears that she and Dante mingled in the same social circle. She married - as did Dante - and she died young at the age of 24, but Dante's affections for her never ended. She was his muse, who inspired the *Vita Nuova* and influenced the *Divine Comedy*.

Vita Nuova means New Life. The work is composed of autobiographical detail and is unique because it is an anthology of poems that are linked by prose which comment on the poems. This literature was part of a new style of writing that blossomed within a circle of Tuscan poets. This new style was termed "stil novo," which means "new style" and it celebrated love. *Stil nova* was not sentimental, but saw love as an absolute ideal, even holy.

Both the *Vita Nuova* and the *Divine Comedy* are filled with symbolism. Very striking is the numerology in both works. It is important to mention this in order to better understand Dante as a poet and the mind behind the poetry, which will give us a deeper appreciation for his art and his illustration of Beatrice. He had a particular attraction to the number 3 and its multiple 9. In the *Vita Nova*, he says he met Beatrice for the first time at the age of 9 and a second time 9 years later at the age of 18 at the 9th hour of the day. Also, the *Divine Comedy* is composed of 3 volumes in which each volume is composed of 33 chapters (not including the introductory chapter in volume one which makes for 100 chapters in the set) and in the narrative, Dante is led by three 3 guides. This emphasis on 3 is clearly intentional. Some, such as Gilbert, have pointed out that *Paradiso* would have been shorter, but it appears that Dante added speeches to the character of Beatrice to complete 33 chapters in *Paradiso* to retain the symbolism and symmetry of the *Divine Comedy*.[37] Some contest that the number 3 honors the Holy Trinity and that the number 9 symbolizes perfection, specifically the perfection of Beatrice. What matters, here, is that Dante intentionally used symbolism to give his poetry deeper and deeper meaning. So, one may ask, "How much is the Beatrice of the *Vita Nova* and the *Divine Comedy* historically accurate and how much is she art?" Dante met Beatrice only twice, so he has little to tell us about her personally, but she was his muse and his feelings for her were very real. I contest that little about Beatrice is historically accurate and that both of the works are high art, but for different reasons. I believe the Beatrice of the *Vita Nuova* is true to Dante's heart. As Singleton explains, "the *Vita Nuova* is beyond any doubt the way of love and not the way of knowledge."[38] And, I believe the Beatrice of the *Divine Comedy* is true to Dante's

[37] Alan H. Gilbert, *Dante and His Comedy* (New York: New York University Press, 1963) 153.

[38] Charles S. Singleton, *An Essay on the Vita Nova* (Baltimore: The John's Hopkins University Press, 1977), 106.

mind in that he structures an allegorical universe where Faith is personified by the love of a beautiful woman. Furthermore, some have pointed out that Beatrice's name is poetically appropriate because it means one who beatifies or one who bestows blessedness. Some have questioned her historical existence, altogether. However, Ferrante suggests that "those who would deny her historicity, like those who reject her allegorical significance, deny the fullness of Dante's poetry."[39] What is important is to recognize the significance of Beatrice in Dante's life and how he was able to express theological truths through her as a character in his art.

In the *Vita Nuova*, Dante's love journey is made up of three parts. The first part describes Dante's encounter with Beatrice and his immediate enamorment of her. The second part describes his desire to establish contact with her that is not external, but internal. The third part is devoted to Dante's love for her on the intellectual level, which moves his love from the earthly to the divine. This last form of love compels "the poet to identify Beatrice with the glory of God once and for all."[40] Singleton explains that Dante's love is like that of a man,

---

[39] Joan M. Ferrante, "Beatrice," in *The Dante Encyclopedia*, ed. Richard Lansing (New York: Garland Publishing, Inc., 2000), 95.
[40] Diana Cavuoto Glenn, "Vita Nuova," in *The Dante Encyclopedia*, ed. Richard Lansing (New York: Garland Publishing, Inc., 2000), 877.

whose love stretches out to Heaven from earth, [which] is precisely the situation of the mystic's love of God. It was an 'excess of the mind,' a 'stretching out of love.' When Augustine and Bonaventura speak of the journey to God, they mean it as a possibility in this life. It is for this reason especially that the pattern of the ascent of love in the *Vita Nuova* can so closely resemble the pattern of the mystic ascent to God."[41]

There is no mistaking Dante's intention to equate his love for Beatrice with the supernatural love of mystics. As I mentioned earlier, in the Middle Ages, the number three, in addition to representing the Holy Trinity, was often used to describe the degrees or levels of the mind and heart's ascent to God. Singleton explains,

> this itinerary of the mind to God, as Augustine had conceived it, began, at its first level, *outside* man. It turned *inward* at its second level or degree. And in its third and last stage, it rose *above* man.[42]

The three parts of the *Vita Nuova* convey this theology effectively. Saint Thomas Aquinas

---

[41] Singleton, *An Essay on the Vita Nuova*,106.
[42] Singleton, *An Essay on the Vita Nuova*, 105-106.

describes the degrees or levels as three lights. Dante uses this same theology in the *Divine Comedy* in the form of three guides. These interpretations come from the same storehouse of theology that bloomed during that era.

Beatrice allegorically represents the middle light - the light of Faith - which descends from the heavens to meet every Christian wayfarer. Beatrice describes to Dante the celestialities of Heaven and all who call it home in a way that he can understand. She says to him,

> This way of speech best suits your apprehension,
> Which knows but to receive reports from sense
> And fit them for the intellect's attention.
> So Scripture stoops to your intelligence:
> It talks about God's 'hand' and 'feet', intending
> That you should draw a different inference.
> And so does holy Church, in pictures lending
> A human face to Michael, Gabriel,
> And him by whom old Tobit found amending
> (*Paradiso,* 4.37-48).[43]

Faith makes the indescribable ascertainable.

---

[43] Dante Alighieri, *The Divine Comedy III: Paradise*, ed. and trans. with notes, by Dorothy L. Sayers, Barbara Reynolds. (London: Penguin Books,1962) 82.

Similarly, so does Scripture and the Church. They describe God's universe in a way that makes it accessible to the human mind.

As Dante journeys from Hell to Heaven, the descriptions of each realm and the theology taught become more abstract. Just as in the narrative, so, too, is the reality of Heaven more enigmatic than the reality of Hell. As the poem moves forward, the more Psalm-like it becomes. For example, when Dante sees God's ineffable magnificence, he says,

> How weak are words, and how unfit to frame
> My concept - which lags after what was shown
> So far, 'twould flatter it to call it lame!
> Eternal light, that in Thyself alone
> Dwelling, alone dost know Thyself, and smile
> On Thy self-love, so knowing and so known!
> (*Paradiso,* 33.121-126).[44]

Ryan explains,

> ... heaven is portrayed predominantly as an extended hymn to the joy experienced as the intellect expands its horizons through increasing knowledge of God and his ways and the will delights in the deeper knowledge

---

[44] Dante Alighieri, *The Divine Comedy III: Paradise*, 346.

thus gained.[45]

Few things bring me greater joy than when I am able to grasp bits of wisdom, grace, faith, revelation and theology - each personified by Beatrice - during my studies. Just as Dante cannot express in words God's magnificence, neither can he express Beatrice's radiance:

> Little by little out of sight withdrew,
> Whence I to Beatrice must needs transfer
> My gaze, for love, and lack of aught to
> view...
> ... Beauty past knowledge was displayed to
> me -
> Not only ours: the joy of it complete
> Her Maker knows, I think, and only He.
> From this point on I must admit defeat
> Sounder than poet wrestling with his theme,
> Comic or tragic, e'er was doomed to meet;
> For her sweet smile remembered, as the beam
> Of sunlight blinds the weakest eyes that gaze,
> Bewilders all my wits and scatters them
> (*Paradiso*, 30.13-27).[46]

---

[45] Christopher Ryan, "Dante Alighieri," in *The Oxford Companion to Christian Thought,* ed. Adrian Hastings, (Oxford: Oxford University Press, 2000), 150.

[46] Dante Alighieri, *The Divine Comedy III: Paradise*, 318-319.

Dante intentionally embodied theology in the figure of Beatrice. His son Pietro pointed out of Beatrice that, "after she died, to enhance the fame of her name, he wanted her to be taken as an allegory and type of theology in this poem."[47] Singleton defines theology as "the science in which first principles are given, not by reason, but through faith and revealed truth."[48] Implying that Beatrice's wisdom is Theology, Virgil tells Dante to wait for Beatrice who will be able to answer his question about the religious phenomenon:

> Now, should my words thy hunger not remove,
> Beatrice shalt thou see, and she'll speak plain,
> This and all cravings else to rid thee of
> (*Purgatorio,* 15.76-78).[49]

As the light of Theology, Beatrice is the source for heavenly answers and as a master teacher to her student Dante, she tests him to see what he has learned during their journey together through Paradise. She herself does not ask him questions; rather, she compels Saint Peter to question Dante:

---

[47] Cited by Joan M. Ferrante, "Beatrice," in *The Dante Encyclopedia*, ed. Richard Lansing (New York: Garland Publishing, Inc., 2000), 91.

[48] Singleton, *Journey to Beatrice*, 23.

[49] Dante Alighieri, *The Divine Comedy II: Purgatory*, 183.

"… Eternal light of that great man
To whom Our Lord on earth bequeathed the keys
Which to this wondrous joy admittance gain,
Lightly and searchingly, as thou dost please,
This person test and try concerning faith,
By which thou once didst walk upon the seas.
If love and hope and faith he truly hath
Thou knowest, for thine eyes are fixed upon
The centre which all visions mirroreth.
Yet since this realm its citizens have won
By the true faith, 'tis fitting he should seek
To glorify it, answering thereon"
(*Paradiso,* 24.36-45). [50]

Confident that he will pass, Beatrice looks on as Dante answers Saint Peter's questions about faith, hope and love.

Since *Inferno's* Canto two, when Beatrice entreats Virgil to guide her friend Dante during his journey through Hell and Purgatory, we have been waiting for Dante and Beatrice's reunion. Sayers explains that at this moment, the,

> literal and allegorical meanings are so closely and intimately fused that it is possible, and at the first reading inevitable, to take it throughout at the purely human level. It is

---

[50] Dante Alighieri, *The Divine Comedy III: Paradise*, 266.

man and a woman meeting, after a long estrangement for which he is to blame; she is justly indignant, and he finds nothing to say for himself. She is the Sacrament of the Body, she is divine Theology, she is the vehicle of Grace, she is the Body of Christ in the Church - but all these identities are summed up in the single identity of her person:

'Look on us well; we are indeed, we are Beatrice…'

Having said that, she has said everything.[51]

So true are Sayers's words. Little is left to say. Beatrice has said it all in one interjection. Once Beatrice has fulfilled her duty to Dante, she leads him to his third and final guide, Saint Bernard, who guides Dante to the Empyrean where God dwells to witness the unmediated vision of God Himself, granted through the gift of what is called the Beatific Vision.

Saint Bernard as an Allegory for the Light of Glory

Dante's third and final guide in the *Divine Comedy* is Saint Bernard. Historically, Saint Bernard was born in Burgundy in 1090. He entered the

---

[51] Dorothy Sayers, Introduction, *The Divine Comedy II: Purgatory,* by Dante Alighieri. ed. and trans. with notes, by Dorothy L. Sayers. (London: Penguin Books, 1949), 27.

Cistercian order at the age of 22 and within a few years he was the founding abbot of Clairvaux. He was a "passionately eloquent spokesman for institutional and intellectual orthodoxy of the staunchest kind" and "probably the most influential individual figure in the twelfth-century church."[52]

In the *Divine Comedy*, Saint Bernard appears in only the final 3 cantos of the entire 100 canto poem. He appears far less than Virgil or Beatrice, yet he is just as symbolically important. Neither Virgil nor Beatrice can lead Dante to the unmediated vision of God. This honor is reserved for a guide of higher esteem, a saint by the name Bernard.

Allegorically, Saint Bernard represents the light of Glory and only with the light of Glory can Dante behold God's Glory. Dante refers to Saint Bernard as "that contemplative soul"[53] teaching us that through contemplation and mysticism, the Christian can encounter God. In practical terms, contemplation coupled with mysticism is prayer. Saint Bernard's chief duty as Dante's guide is to intercede for him and pray to the Virgin Mother for the Grace needed to behold God. With humility and adoration, Saint Bernard pleads,

---

[52] Steven Botterill, "Bernard, St.," in *The Dante Encyclopedia*, ed. Richard Lansing (New York: Garland Publishing, Inc., 2000), 99.
[53] Dante Alighieri, *The Divine Comedy III: Paradise*, 334.

O Virgin Mother, Daughter of thy Son...

This man, who witnessed from the deepest pit
Of all the universe, up to this height,
The souls' lives one by one, doeth now entreat
That thou, by grace, may grant to him such
might
That higher yet in vision he may rise
Towards the final source of bliss and light
(*Paradiso*, 33.1-27).[54]

So, too, must the Christian wayfarer pray - with humility and adoration - if he seeks God, which Saint Thomas calls "patria" meaning home because it is in God that the soul is at home.

Saint Bernard is a representative for all the saints. Each one represents the light of Glory. Christians can be filled with Faith, but the saints are not normal Christians because they are filled with God's Glory. They are blessed with the gift of Beatific Vision to witness the unmediated vision of God Himself. It is a gift reserved for them because of their devotion to God. The protagonist Dante is allowed to see what the saints see because a saint is his guide.

The saints dwell in God's unmitigated love. Furthest from the saints and God's love is Satan who resides at the bottom of Hell's pit. He is frozen to his

---

[54] Dante Alighieri, *The Divine Comedy III: Paradise*, 343-344.

waist in ice. Hell is the coldest place in the universe, so cold that the condemned - isolated from each other and alone - cannot move or speak. The exception is Satan who beats his bat-like wings keeping Hell and all the condemned forever frozen. Heaven is the opposite. It is at the highest of highests where space and time do not exist. It is a bright comforting euphoric community. God dwells in the Empyrean with the angels and saints who sit on the petals of a snow-white rose. God's everlasting love is everywhere and in everything. What is better than love? Nothing. It is free, yet the most valuable thing in the universe. This is the reason why Dante wrote the poem, so we would journey toward God's light, warmth and love. Satan's torture is not the darkness or cold. It is the madness and insanity that drowns him because he will never again see God. He will never again be comforted by Him or be a part of His love. There is no place worse than Hell because it is a place without God.

Conclusion

In this paper, we have investigated the *Divine Comedy's* allegorical nature, specifically Dante's three guides who represent the three lights that guide humankind to God. The light of Reason personified by Virgil, the light of Faith personified by Beatrice and the light of Glory personified by Saint Bernard lead to the Supreme Light that is God. Each of the minor lights is a radiance or reflection of the Greater Light. By witnessing God's Supreme Light, Dante is "transformed." He explains,

> That light doth so transform a man's whole bent
> That never to another sight or thought
> Would he surrender, with his own consent;
> For everything the will has ever sought
> Is gathered there, and there is every quest
> Made perfect, which apart from it falls short
> (*Paradiso*, 33.100-105).[55]

So, too, are the experiences of the saints in our world. The saints in this world devote their lives to God because nothing else compares to Him. All else is superfluous in comparison to God, who alone is worthy of adoration and adulation. Every Christian in this world is called to become a saint. Dante's encounter with God is meant to be the goal for every Christian, but each Christian must seek it and journey toward it in order to experience it.

---

[55] Dante Alighieri, *The Divine Comedy III: Paradise*, 346.

Bibliography

Bloom, Harold, ed. *Dante's Divine Comedy*. New York: Chelsea House Publishers, 1987.

Botterill, Steven. "Bernard, St." In *The Dante Encyclopedia*, ed. Richard Lansing, 99-100. New York: Garland Publishing, Inc., 2000.

Crissman, Charley. "The Tragedy of Virgil." (18 January 2011). http://www.gmalivuk.com/otherstuff/otherpeople/charley_Tragedyvirgil.html

Dante Alighieri. *The Divine Comedy I: Hell*, ed. and trans. with notes, by Dorothy L. Sayers. London: Penguin Books, 1949.

_____. *The Divine Comedy II: Purgatory*, ed. and trans. with notes, by Dorothy L. Sayers. London: Penguin Books, 1955.

_____. *The Divine Comedy III: Paradise*, ed. and trans. with notes, by Dorothy L. Sayers, Barbara Reynolds. London: Penguin Books, 1962.

_____. *La Vita Nuova*, ed. and trans. with notes, by Barbara Reynolds. London: Penguin Books, 1969.

Ferrante, Joan M. "Beatrice." In *The Dante Encyclopedia*, ed. Richard Lansing, 89-95. New York: Garland Publishing, Inc., 2000.

Gilbert, Allan H. *Dante and His Comedy*. New York: New York University Press, 1963.

Glazov, Gregory. "The Spiritual Journey in Dante's Vita Nuova." A Microsoft Office PowerPoint presentation. South Orange, New Jersey. 18 January 2011.

_____. "The Spiritual Journey in the Divine Comedy." A Microsoft Office PowerPoint presentation. South Orange, New Jersey. 18 January 2011.

_____. "The Spiritual Journey in the Divine Comedy Part II: The Three Lights." A Microsoft Office PowerPoint presentation. South Orange, New Jersey. 18 January 2011.

_____. "The Spiritual Journey in Dante's Divine Comedy, Final Part." A Microsoft Office PowerPoint presentation. South Orange, New Jersey. 18 January 2011.

Glenn, Diana Cavuoto. "Vita Nuova." In *The Dante Encyclopedia*, ed. Richard Lansing, 874-878.

New York: Garland Publishing, Inc., 2000.

Hatzfeld, Helmut. Review of *Journey to Beatrice*, by Charles S. Singleton. *Modern Language Journal*, vol. 43, no. 7 (Nov. 1959): 354-55.

Hollander, Robert. *Dante: A Life in Works*. New Haven: Yale University Press, 2001.

_____. "Dante's Virgil: A Light That Failed." 1989. *Lectura Dantis: Online.* (18 January 2011). http://www.brown.edu/Departments/Italian_St udies/LD/numbers/04/hollander.html

_____. "Virgil." In *The Dante Encyclopedia*, ed. Richard Lansing, 862-865. New York: Garland Publishing, Inc., 2000.

Pellegrini, Anthony L. Review of *Further Papers on Dante*, by Dorothy L. Sayers. *Speculum*, vol. 35, no. 1 (Jan. 1960): 142-44.

Quinones, Ricardo J. *Dante Alighieri*. New York: Twayne Publishers, 1998.

Reynolds, Barbara. Introduction. *The Divine Comedy III: Paradise.* by Dante Alighieri. ed. and trans. with notes, by Dorothy L. Sayers, Barbara Reynolds. London: Penguin Books,

1962. 17-51.

Ryan, Christopher. "Dante Alighieri." In *The Oxford companion to Christian Thought,* ed. Adrian Hastings, 149-151. Oxford: Oxford University Press, 2000.

Sayers, Dorothy L. Introduction. *The Divine Comedy I: Hell.* by Dante Alighieri. ed. and trans. with notes, by Dorothy L. Sayers. London: Penguin Books, 1949. 9-69.

_____. Introduction. *The Divine Comedy II: Purgatory.* by Dante Alighieri. ed. and trans. with notes, by Dorothy L. Sayers. London: Penguin Books, 1955. 9-71.

_____. *Further Papers on Dante.* London: Methuen and Co., 1957.

_____. *Introductory Papers on Dante.* London: Methuen and Co., 1954.

Schnapp, Jeffrey T. "Purgatorio." In *The Dante Encyclopedia*, ed. Richard Lansing, 723-728. New York: Garland Publishing, Inc., 2000.

Singleton, Charles S. *Journey to Beatrice.* Baltimore: The John's Hopkins University Press, 1977.

_____. *An Essay on the Vita Nova.*
Baltimore: The John's Hopkins University
Press, 1977.

"Virgil's Role in the Divine Comedy." *Dante and
Virgil: A Study of Poetry, Language and
History.* (18 January 2011).
http://users.rcn.com/antos/dante/divine_com.h
tml

HIERARCHY OF TRUTHS

JAMES THOMAS ANGELIDIS

The following is my graduate school paper about the expression, "hierarchy of truths," which reached a mass audience in Catholic Vatican Council II's decree on Christian ecumenism.

On November 21, 1964, Vatican Council II promulgated a special decree on ecumenism, *Unitatis redintegratio*. It noted that among the various Christian denominations there exist differences concerning doctrine, discipline and church structure; however, the decree emphasized that these present-day divisions contradict Christ's will and it emphasized the unifying elements of the Christian denominations. At the Council, observers attended representing the Orthodox churches, various Protestant denominations, the Anglican Church and members of the World Council of Churches. They had access to all the documents given to the Council Fathers and were present at all of the general sessions. Although, they were not allowed to speak or vote during the Council, their presence furthered the Council's ecumenical mission.[56] Congar asserts that the Decree on Ecumenism "ranks among the great documents of Christian history."[57] The expression "hierarchy of truths" thundered in the document and has echoed since it was penned almost fifty years ago and it has tremendous potential for ecumenism among Christians. Reamonin declared it as, "one of the great insights of Vatican II."[58] Cullman proclaimed the hierarchy of truths passage "the most revolutionary" of all 16 Vatican II documents.[59] This paper will be an investigation into the expression, "hierarchy of truths."

The Decree on Ecumenism states,

In ecumenical dialogue, Catholic theologians standing fast by the teaching of the Church and investigating the divine mysteries with the

---

[56] M. Browne, E. Duff, J. Ford, V. Lafontaine, "Ecumenical Movement," in *New Catholic Encyclopedia*, 2nd ed., ed. Berard Marthaler, (Washington: Gale, 2003), 74-75.

[57] Yves Congar, *Diversity and Communion* (Mystic: Twenty-Third Publications, 1985), 126.

[58] Vincent Twomey, "'Hierarchy' of Truths," *The Furrow*, vol. 42, no. 9 (September, 1991): 500.

[59] Tom Stransky, "Hierarchy of Truths," in *Dictionary of the Ecumenical Movement,* ed. Nicholas Lossky (Geneva: WCC Publications, 2002), 519.

separated brethren must proceed with love for the truth, with charity, and with humility. When comparing doctrines with one another, they should remember that in Catholic doctrine there exists a "hierarchy" of truths, since they vary in their relation to the fundamental Christian faith. Thus, the way will be opened by which through fraternal rivalry all will be stirred to a deeper understanding and a clearer presentation of the unfathomable riches of Christ.[60]

Though the expression "hierarchy of truths" received its greatest attention during Vatican II, it was originated in 1963 in a speech by Archbishop Andrea Pangrazio of Gorizia, Italy. In the speech, he explains that God's divine dynamism can change the course of history and that "God can make possible that desired union of separate Christianities which today still seems impossible. This will be possible, however, only if all Christians will be obedient to inspirations of divine grace."[61] He explains there are common elements among the Christian denominations, but to list them would be to pile them up in quantitative fashion. He believes we "should point to the *center*,

---

[60] Decree on Ecumenism, *Unitatis reintegratio*. Vatican II, November 21, 1964 (2.11).

[61] Andre Pangrazio, "The Mystery of the History of the Church," in *Council Speeches of Vatican II*, ed. H. Kung, Y. Congar & D. O'Hanlon (New York: Paulist Press, 1964), 190.

to which all these elements are related, and without which they cannot be explained. This bond and center is Christ himself, whom all Christians acknowledge as Lord of the Church."[62] Because there is unity and diversity among Christians, it is very important "to pay close attention to the *hierarchical order* of revealed truths which express the mystery of Christ."[63] The expression "hierarchy of truths" has appeared in many sources since Pangrazio first introduced it in 1963. Some will be referred to below.

The Catholic Church has not created an official rank or list of the hierarchy of truths because, as Cardinal Ratzinger explained, "What the term hierarchy of truths seeks to express is that the faith of the Church is… an organic whole in which every individual element obtains its meaning from being seen from within its proper place within the whole."[64] According to the *Catechism of the Catholic Church*, the center of this organic whole is the mystery of the Most Holy Trinity:

> It is the mystery of God in himself. It is
> therefore the source of all the other mysteries

---

[62] Pangrazio, "The Mystery of the History of the Church," 190-191.

[63] Pangrazio, "The Mystery of the History of the Church," 191.

[64] Christopher O'Donnell, "Hierarchy of Truths," in *Ecclesia: A Theological Encyclopedia of the Church.* ed. Michael Glazier (Collegeville: Liturgical Press, 1996) 195-196.

of faith, the light that enlightens them. It is the most fundamental and essential teaching in the "hierarchy of the truths of faith."[56] The whole history of salvation is identical with the history of the way and the means by which the one true God, Father, Son and Holy Spirit, reveals himself to men "and reconciles and unites with himself those who turn away from sin"[65]

Congar was an early champion for ecumenism and the theology behind "hierarchy of truths." He explains, "Catholic doctrine is organized rather like a tree, the smallest branches of which are connected to the trunk by the others... Everything is attached to one foundation (a trunk), which is the mystery of Christ the savior, presupposing the mystery of the triunity of God."[66] The centrality of Christ "is not opposed to the trinitarian view; it is through the Incarnation of the Eternal son, his life, death and Resurrection, that the Father is revealed and the Spirit is given. Therefore, catechesis, to be trinitarian, has to be Christocentric."[67] More comprehensively, the *General Catechetical Directory* explains that the hierarchy of truths:

---

[65] *Catechism of the Catholic Church*, 234.

[66] Congar, *Diversity and Communion*, 128.

[67] Joseph Ratzinger. Christoph Schonborn, *Introduction to the Catechism of the Catholic Church* (San Francisco: Ignatius Press, 1994), 44-45.

may be grouped under four basic heads: the mystery of God the Father, the Son, and the Holy Spirit, Creator of all things; the mystery of Christ the incarnate Word, who was born of the Virgin Mary, and who suffered, died, and rose for our salvation; the mystery of the Holy Spirit, who is present in the Church, sanctifying it and guiding it until the glorious coming of Christ, our Savior and Judge; and the mystery of the Church, which is Christ's Mystical Body, in which the Virgin Mary holds the preeminent place.[68]

This teaching is most visible in The Nicene-Constantinopolitan Creed of 381, which is central and fundamental to the Catholic Faith and must be accepted for ecumenism.

The Catholic Church teaches that all doctrinal teachings of the Church are true and that no truth is dispensable. "From a purely intellectual and logical point of view, any true statement of whatever kind is equal to another true statement. The character of truth is an absolute, which as such and in a formal way, cannot be either more or less true. From this point of view there can be no degrees in truth."[69]

---

[68] Sacred Congregation for the Clergy, *General Catechetical Directory*, 1971 (43).

[69] Congar, *Diversity and Communion*, 129.

However, Pangrazio explains that "although all the truths revealed by divine faith are to be believed with the same divine faith and all those elements which make up the Church must be kept with equal fidelity, not all of them are of equal importance."[70] In the hierarchy, no truths "pertain to faith itself less than others, but rather that some truths are based on others as of higher priority, and are illumined by them."[71] For example, the doctrine that Mary is the Mother God is unimaginable without understanding the doctrine that Jesus is both true God and true man. This latter doctrine about Jesus is higher in the hierarchy of truths and it illumines the teaching about Mary. Similarly, the doctrine of the two natures of Christ illumines the doctrine on the human and divine wills of Christ; the former doctrine has a higher priority in the hierarchy of truths.[72] The importance of each truth depends on how close it is to the Church's most fundamental teaching, "which is the mystery of Christ the savior, presupposing the mystery of the triunity of God."[73] Therefore, "grace has more importance than sin, sanctifying grace more than actual grace, the resurrection of Christ more than

---

[70] Pangrazio, "The Mystery of the History of the Church," 191.

[71] Sacred Congregation for the Clergy, *General Catechetical Directory*, 1971 (43).

[72] Douglas Bushman, "Understanding the Hierarchy of Truths." January 2000, available from http://www.ignatiusinsight.com/features2005/dbushman_hiertruths_sept05.asp. Internet; accessed 15 March 2013.

his childhood, the mystical aspect of the church more than its juridical; the church's liturgy more than private devotions."[74] The central truths "which all other truths are ordered consists of those basic truths, each of which evokes the others and cannot be reduced to some other."[75] The criteria to establish a hierarchy of truths comes from "Scripture, tradition, creeds, the Fathers, liturgy, official Church teaching and [the sense of faith]."[76] "Many of the most central truths of the faith, Christians are already one."[77]

All Christian statements "are either statements strictly concerned with Christ or derivative from such statements; in each case there are various grades... logically speaking, the hierarchy of truths is not a matter of demoting some truths, but rather concerns more carefully identifying the exact content of faith statements."[78] Some truths are less important, but no truth can be subtracted. As explained in the *Introduction to the Catechism of the Catholic Church*, "the 'hierarchy of truth' does not mean 'a principle of subtraction,' as if faith could be reduced to some 'essentials' whereas the 'rest' is left free or even

---

[73] Congar, *Diversity and Communion*, 128.

[74] Stransky, "Hierarchy of Truths," 519.

[75] William Henn, "The Hierarchy of Truths Twenty Years Later," *Theological Studies*, no. 48 (1987): 464.

[76] Henn, "The Hierarchy of Truths Twenty Years Later," 462.

[77] Henn, "The Hierarchy of Truths Twenty Years Later," 468.

[78] Henn, "The Hierarchy of Truths Twenty Years Later," 449.

dismissed as not significant. The 'hierarchy of truth' … is a principle of organic structure. It should not be confused with the degrees of certainty; it simply means that the different truths of faith are 'organized' around a center."[79] There is an interconnectedness and interdependence of the different truths: "the highest does not stand without the lowest though it is possible and necessary to distinguish between them."[80] The purpose of the hierarchy of truths is "not to separate non-negotiable fundamental articles from optional non-fundamental articles of faith. Rather it interprets and brings perspective into the whole body of truths."[81] No truths can be can be isolated because they are a part of a harmonious whole. "As in a piece of music, one wrong note can mar the whole. So too the truths of Faith and those of morals form a symphonic whole whose expression is liturgy, worship of God."[82] "They support one another, illuminate one another, complement one another. The principle of the hierarchy of truths is not meant to violate in any way the deposit of revelation."[83] Furthermore, Congar believes that "no truth contradicts another truth. If there appears to be

---

[79] Ratzinger, *Introduction to the Catechism of the Catholic Church*, 42.

[80] Twomey, "'Hierarchy' of Truths," 502.

[81] Henn, "The Hierarchy of Truths Twenty Years Later," 443.

[82] Twomey, "'Hierarchy' of Truths," 503.

such a contradiction, there has been some misunderstanding. This triumph of the consistency of truth allows for... an exuberant acceptance of the true affirmations of other Christian Churches, of world religions and of humanity in general."[84]

Cardona believes that faith is necessary for recognizing truths and their order. He asserts, as summarized by Henn, that,

> revealed truth is never a deduction from what is known through reason. Rather, it is known through an obedient faith to the authority of God. [Cardona] then relates the truth known in faith to truth as such. Truth is always in a way secondary to reality, insofar as it signifies the intellect's adequation to reality. As such, truth does not admit of being "more" or "less." One either knows reality or one does not. In considering any order among the truths, it is important to realize that one must accept the *totality* of what God reveals and that one must do so because of the authority of God who reveals.[85]

---

[83] William Henn, *The Hierarchy of Truths According to Yves Congar*. (Rome: Editrice Pontificia Universita Gregoriana, 1987), 209.

[84] Henn, *The Hierarchy of Truths According to Yves Congar*, 210.

[85] Henn, "The Hierarchy of Truths Twenty Years Later," 456.

Therefore, faith in God and what He reveals is essential to understanding the order of truths.

Though the expression "hierarchy of truths" was brought to the world's attention at Vatican II, the theology behind it is not completely new. In the Old Testament, prophets and rabbis were known to provide summaries or "cores" of the Law. For example, Hillel famously taught, "What is hateful to you, do not do to your neighbor; that is the whole Torah, while the rest is commentary thereof." Similarly, when Jesus was asked, "Teacher, which is the great commandment in the law?" he answered, "You shall love the Lord your God with all your heart, and with all your soul, and with all your mind. This is the great and first commandment. And a second is like it, you shall love your neighbor as yourself. On these two commandments depend all the law and the prophets."[86] Both Hillel and Jesus focused on the weightier matters and created a hierarchy of truths in their teachings.[87] We see in the New Testament, further latent forms of a hierarchy of truths in the words of the Apostle Paul: "So faith, hope, love abide, these three; but the greatest of these is love."[88] In addition, "For I delivered to you as of first importance what I also received, that Christ died

---

[86] Matthew 22:36-40, RSV.

[87] William McFadden, "Hierarchy of Truths" in *The Modern Catholic, Encyclopedia*, ed. Michael Glazier (Collegeville: Liturgical Press, 1994), 360.

[88] 1 Corinthians 13:13, RSV.

for our sins in accordance with the scriptures, that he was buried, that he was raised on the third day in accordance with the scriptures, and that he appeared to Cephas, then to the twelve."[89] In the fourteenth century, in William of Ockham's *Dialogus adversus haereticos*, an anonymous author writes, "The only truths that are to be considered Catholic and necessary to salvation are explicitly or implicitly stated in the cannon of the Bible... All other truths... are not to be held as Catholic, even if they are stated in the writings of the Fathers or the definitions of the supreme pontiffs, and even if they are believed by all the faithful. To assent to them... is not necessary to salvation."[90] Here, as the author stresses, a hierarchy of truths can only be derived from the Bible. Not all may accept his theology, but it is further evidence of a hierarchy of truths in the making. In the sixteenth century, Luther, grasping the relationship between scripture and what is apostolic, asserts that "the apostolic element in scripture is what speaks of Christ, my saviour. The criterion of apostolic authenticity is '*to preach and convey Christ.*' Whatever does not teach Christ is not apostolic, though it come from Peter or Paul; by contrast whatever preaches Christ is apostolic, even if it comes from Judas, from Annas, from Pilate or from

---

[89] 1 Corinthians 15:3-5, RSV.
[90] George Tavard, "'Hierarchia Veritatum' A Preliminary Investigation." *Theological Studies*, no.32 (1971): 286.

Herod."[91] Here, Luther has developed a criterion to decipher what is valuable. It is an example of what is the core in his faith. The idea of a hierarchy of truths is there in Luther's words, which makes dialogue possible. Later on in the sixteenth century, Calvin said, "For all the heads of true doctrine are not in the same position. Some are so necessary to be known, that all must hold them to be fixed and undoubted as the proper essentials for religion: for instance that God is one, that Christ is God, and the Son of God, that our salvation depends on the mercy of God, and the like. Others again, which are the subject of controversy among the churches, do not destroy the unity of the faith."[92] Almost 500 years before Vatican II, the theology of a hierarchy of truths is evident in Calvin's teachings. Like the Protestant theologians, the Orthodox theologians have a sense of a hierarchy of truths. As Congar explains, "Orthodoxy spontaneously re-attaches to their center all the elements of revelation, following the genius of the Fathers of the Church... Everything - including the most concrete details of life - is always rooted in the trinitarian center and illumined by it."[93] Congar also explains, "The East takes its stand on the Fathers and the Ecumenical Councils, which have stated the

---

[91] Congar, *Diversity and Communion*, 128.

[92] Henn, *The Hierarchy of Truths According to Yves Congar*, 174.

[93] Henn, *The Hierarchy of Truths According to Yves Congar*, 175.

essentials."[94] The fundamentals of Orthodox theology come from the Church Fathers and first seven Ecumenical Councils, fundamentals that are shared by Catholics and most Protestants.

The above examples show that, throughout history, attempts have been made to form a hierarchy of truths in the Christian denominations. With the rise of the ecumenical movement in the past century, the Vatican II Fathers were called to follow the above examples and focus on the weightier matters for the sake of fruitful dialogue. The workings of a hierarchy of truths have come from the past and will continue into the future. As Congar explains, faith in God,

> is drawn out into certain content, in affirmations and judgments, into which it becomes diversified. It is diversified in time, which has an effect on its formulation ("Christ will come," "Christ has come"); it is diversified into various articles or dogmas which are worked out over the course of time: those of the creed, those of the councils, those which have been possible to add already or those which will be added in the future"[95]

---

[94] Henn, *The Hierarchy of Truths According to Yves Congar*, 176.

[95] Henn, *The Hierarchy of Truths According to Yves Congar*, 169.

The Catholic Church has taken the first step toward ecumenism. Henn explains that "from a kind but one-sided call to return home, the Catholic Church moved to recognition of elements of salvation in other Churches. With the hierarchy of truths doctrine, the Catholic Church took another step forward and recognized an order within its own teachings, placing Christ at the foundation. This was an important move toward a better perspective. The hierarchy of truths should function as a hermeneutical principle. However, one should expect from this teaching not a quick unity but rather a growth in mutual understanding about the agreements and differences between Christians."[96] The hierarchy of truths is "an invitation and stimulus to further thought on the focus of faith."[97]

Congar is very important in the effort for ecumenism. He devoted his life to it. As he says, "The very idea of diversity compatible with communion, or of the necessary but sufficient minimum of common doctrine to be held if unity is to be preserved, is in fact the object of all my research."[98] In his theology, he makes a distinction between the perspective of the object known and the

---

[96] Henn, *The Hierarchy of Truths According to Yves Congar*, 217.

[97] Denis Carroll, "'Hierarchia Veritatum': A Theological and Pastoral Insight of the Second Vatican Council," *Irish Theological Quarterly*, no. 44 (1977): 129

[98] Henn, *The Hierarchy of Truths According to Yves Congar*, 198.

perspective of the knowing subject. The objects known are directly related to the foundation, core, nucleus, heart of the Christianity, "which is the mystery of Christ the savior, presupposing the mystery of the triunity of God."[99] All truths rely on this foundation. Suppositions that do not rely on this foundation are not truths and they can be seen in schools of indifferentism, bad liberalism and radical pluralism.[100] He believes that "the hierarchy of truths is not a 'creation' of the knower. The order among truths is not imposed by the subject but the reality." Revelation is God's self-manifestation and "revelation allows the believer to know reality from the perspective of God." Order is derived from that which is revealed by God who "alone is absolute truth." One can only know certain aspects of God's truth. "God's view is the final court of appeals. This view is imparted to us to some degree in revelation."[101]

In Congar's theology, the perspective of the knowing subject is just as critical as the perspective of the object known in deciphering a hierarchy of truths. The perspective of the knowing subject must be investigated through a historical lens. Any method that does not must be rejected. The study of the

---

[99] Congar, *Diversity and Communion*, 128.

[100] Henn, *The Hierarchy of Truths According to Yves Congar*, 209.

[101] Henn, *The Hierarchy of Truths According to Yves Congar*, 202.

historicity of the knowing subject can also be referred to as hermeneutics. "The hierarchy of truths might thus serve as a hermeneutical principle for appropriating historically the Christian tradition and for guiding contemporary subjects in their expression of that tradition."[102] The hierarchy of truths positively assesses diversity and unity in the knowing subjects. Mere pluralism is not the answer because unity is also desired. Neither is mere unity the answer because that would undermine legitimate pluralism. "Legitimate pluralism contributes to a fuller grasp of the truth."[103] Significantly, the hierarchy of truths is fundamentally integrated with the magisterium. "The hierarchy of truths helps make evident one of the reasons why an authoritative teaching office is needed - i.e. to determine with the help of the Holy Spirit what the central truths of the faith are." The magisterium "provides guidance on both more central and less central matters." It is essential in determining what qualifies as a truth. The magisterium's teachings make evident that there is a hierarchy of truths. It helps the faithful contemplate scripture and tradition to make discernible what God reveals to the individual and the community as a whole.[104]

---

[102] Henn, *The Hierarchy of Truths According to Yves Congar*, 210.

[103] Henn, *The Hierarchy of Truths According to Yves Congar*, 210.

[104] Henn, *The Hierarchy of Truths According to Yves Congar*, 211.

The perspective of the object known and the perspective of the knowing subject are both necessary to define truths. As Henn explains,

> Object and subject correlate. Neither are able to be taken out of the act of knowing in faith the truths God has revealed. One would expect, therefore, that the hierarchy of truths from the perspective of the object is conditioned by the hierarchy of truths from the perspective of the subject, and vice versa. Thus, the hierarchy obtaining among the truths is knowable only by the adequate subject of those truths, the Church guided by the Holy Spirit. Conversely, there are more important and less important elements in subjective expressions of the faith precisely because there is an objective hierarchy among the truths of revelation.[105]

Congar believes that in the past, the object known was the focus, while in the modern era, the knowing subject is the focus. However, because of Congar and through the hierarchy of truths, it is evident that both object and subject work together.

Truths in Catholic doctrine tend to fall into two categories: those on our final goal and those as a means to salvation. This theology was presented in

---

[105] Henn, *The Hierarchy of Truths According to Yves Congar*, 197.

Archbishop Pangrazio's 1963 speech. In the speech, he explains:

> Some truths are *on the level of our final goal*, such as the mystery of the Blessed Trinity, the Incarnation and Redemption, God's love and mercy toward sinful humanity, eternal life in the perfect kingdom of God, and others.
>
> Other truths are *on the level of means toward salvation*, such as that there are seven sacraments, truths concerning the hierarchical structure of the Church, the apostolic succession, and others. These truths concern the means which are given by Christ to the Church for her pilgrim journey here on earth; when this journey comes to an end, so also do these means.
>
> Now doctrinal differences among Christians have less to do with these primary truths on the level of our final goal, and deal mostly with truths on the level of means, which are certainly subordinate to those other primary truths.
>
> But we can say that the unity of Christians consists in a common faith and belief in those truths which concern our final goal.[106]

---

[106] Pangrazio, "The Mystery of the History of the Church," 191-192.

Taravad explains that the truths pertaining to our final goal will last in heaven, while the truths pertaining to the means of our salvation will disappear with present world.[107] Leeming believes that for fruitful ecumenical dialogue, Christians should pay more attention to the truths regarding the final goal of which there is already a sense of unity. Of secondary concern should be truths pertaining to the means of salvation, which divide the various Christian churches.[108]

There is a clear and rational reason for diversity among Christians and the churches, according to Congar. He explains that human beings have a limited perception of what is truth. It is developed in the mind. Only the Father, Son and Holy Spirit can perceive supernatural truth perfectly. Here on earth, supernatural truth is subject to historicity, which imposes limits on it. Therefore, naturally, supernatural truth is subject to differences in the perception and expression between different churches or even in different periods in one church. "In these expressions we necessarily find particular elements of culture, language and vocabulary, and of common philosophy. Thus a human element of interpretation, systematization and expression is

---

[107] Tavard, "'Hierarchia Veritatum' A Preliminary Investigation," 281.
[108] Tavard, "'Hierarchia Veritatum' A Preliminary Investigation," 283.

combined with the perception of faith which may become dogma." The differences of dogma show that there are different forms of a hierarchy of truths materializing from the objective supernatural form.[109] This is in line with Saint Thomas's "God-centered view of revelation which identifies religious truth ultimately with the outlook of God, never fully graspable by us and therefore calling for modesty in our truth claims and acceptance of legitimate diversity."[110]

Each of the Christian Churches should create a hierarchy of truths and as they do, it is expected that results will have some differences, but this should be no cause for alarm. As Cullman explains, as summarized by Henn, "Just as the Holy Spirit is the source of diverse charisms, so too is the Holy Spirit the source of various accentuations and perspectives in the understanding of the faith on the part of the various Churches. Uniformity is a sin against the Holy Spirit who always works by diversifying." Diversity is only a problem when there is no common ground. The task is to establish a foundation, so the churches can take a closer look at the differences and see how they relate to the foundation and each other. Differences are fine as long as all accept the foundation. "The differences between the hierarchies of truths expressed by the various Churches need not

---

[109] Congar, *Diversity and Communion*, 130.
[110] Henn, *The Hierarchy of Truths According to Yves Congar*, 230.

be divisive but can be complementary." Dialogue is essential and the various Churches can learn from each other; however, it is important to not isolate any doctrine. "Doctrines isolated from the whole tend to usurp the place for fundamental truths. The result is often heresy."[111]

Even if there is direct opposition between two Churches regarding a particular truth, ecumenism should still be pursued. Cullman points out Apostle Paul's advice about the question of eating food sacrificed to idols[112]:

> I know and am persuaded in the Lord Jesus that nothing is unclean in itself; but it is unclean for anyone who thinks it unclean. If your brother is being injured by what you eat, you are no longer walking in love. Do not let what you eat cause the ruin of one for whom Christ died. So do not let your good be spoken of as evil. For the kingdom of God is not food and drink but righteousness and peace and joy in the Holy Spirit; he who thus serves Christ is acceptable to God and approved by men.[113]

---

[111] Henn, *The Hierarchy of Truths According to Yves Congar*, 232.
[112] Henn, "The Hierarchy of Truths Twenty Years Later," 465.
[113] Romans 14:14-18, RSV.

Here, it is clear that Paul wants to unite his brethren and tries to persuade them to focus on the higher truth in the faith to live in "righteousness and peace and joy in the Holy Spirit" and not harm each other on a lesser truth about unclean foods. Cullmann believes that though one should not yield in proclaiming Christian truths, "there is no unity without some concessions"[114] and that "not only a variety of perspectives but even some opposition about less fundamental truths should be tolerated with love."[115]

Much of Vatican II was about the Catholic Church applying its teachings to a new era. The Council stood on the Church's past theology and applied it to the modern world. It was about renewal. It respected the past, while looking to the future. The hierarchy of truths is a perfect example of this dynamism. In the past, Jesus and Paul taught a hierarchy of truths and then Vatican II reaffirmed its importance for our age. The hierarchy of truths is a powerful tool to produce fruitful ecumenical dialogue. Although it has not fully matured, it has immense potential for ecumenism. Through it, Christians will see that we have more in common than not. All who believe in the Father, Son and Holy Spirit are already one. Our beliefs in the means of salvation must not supersede our beliefs on our final

---

[114] Henn, *The Hierarchy of Truths According to Yves Congar*, 234.

[115] Henn, *The Hierarchy of Truths According to Yves Congar*, 232.

goal. Should differences in methods of fasting separate Christians? I think not. Does believing that Jesus is "the way, and the truth, and the life" unite Christians?[116] Indeed, it does. Though there may be diversity in our Christian community, we are all Christians. Diversity must not divide us. We must look beyond it, if not embrace it. I believe ecumenism is near. In 2001, Pope John Paul II sorrowfully apologized on behalf of the Catholic Church to Ecumenical Patriarch Bartholomew I of Constantinople for the sacking of Constantinople in 1204 by Catholic Crusaders. The sack of Constantinople has been seen as the final act of the East-West Schism; however, Pope John Paul II's apology can be the beginning of ecumenism between the Catholic Church and the Orthodox Church. Furthermore, about a month ago, Ecumenical Patriarch Bartholomew I celebrated and attended Pope Francis's Inauguration as the leader of the Catholic Church. If an 800 year old rift between the Catholic Church and the Orthodox Church can be mended, there is hope for ecumenism for all the Christian Churches. We must set aside our differences and focus on the weightier matters. We must not allow our worldly agendas prevent us from attaining our heavenly goals. We have great things in common and I see this more clearly than ever before

---

[116] John 14:6, RSV.

because of my investigation into the expression, "hierarchy of truths."

Works Cited

Browne, M, E. Duff, J. Ford, V. Lafontaine.
    "Ecumenical Movement." In *New Catholic
    Encyclopedia, 2nd ed.* ed. Berard Marthaler,
    74-75. Washington: Gale, 2003.

Bushman, Douglas. "Understanding the Hierarchy of
    Truths." January 2000. Available from
    http://www.ignatiusinsight.com/features2005/
    dbushman_hiertruths_sept05.asp. Internet;
    accessed 15 March 2013.

Carroll, Denis. "'Hierarchia Veritatum': A
    Theological and Pastoral Insight of the Second
    Vatican Council." *Irish Theological
    Quarterly*, no. 44 (1977): 125-133.

Catechism of the Catholic Church. New York:
    Doubleday, 1995 (234).

Congar, Yves. *Diversity and Communion.* Mystic:
    Twenty-Third Publications, 1985.

Decree on Ecumenism, *Unitatis reintegratio.* Vatican
    II, November 21, 1964 (2.11).
    http://www.vatican.va/archive/hist_councils/ii
    _vatican_council/documents/vat-
    ii_decree_19641121_unitatis-
    redintegratio_en.html.

Ford, J.T. "Hierarchy of Truths." In *New Catholic Encyclopedia, 2nd ed.* ed. Berard Marthaler, 822. Washington: Gale, 2003.

Henn, William. *The Hierarchy of Truths According to Yves Congar.* Rome: Editrice Pontificia Universita Gregoriana, 1987.

Henn, William. "The Hierarchy of Truths Twenty Years Later." *Theological Studies*, no. 48 (1987): 439-471.

McFadden, William. "Hierarchy of Truths." In *The Modern Catholic Encyclopedia*, ed. Michael Glazier, 360. Collegeville: Liturgical Press, 1994.

O'Donnell, Christopher. "Hierarchy of Truths." In *Ecclesia: A Theological Encyclopedia of the Church.* ed. Michael Glazier, 195-196, Collegeville: Liturgical Press, 1996.

Pangrazio, Andre. "The Mystery of the History of the Church." In *Council Speeches of Vatican II*, ed. H. Kung, Y. Congar & D. O'Hanlon, 188-92. New York: Paulist Press, 1964.

Ratzinger, Joseph, Christoph Schonborn. *Introduction to the Catechism of the Catholic*

Church. San Francisco: Ignatius Press, 1994.

Sacred Congregation for the Clergy, *General Catechetical Directory*, 1971 (43). http://www.papalencyclicals.net/Paul06/gencatdi.htm.

Stransky, Tom. "Hierarchy of Truths." In *Dictionary of the Ecumenical Movement,* ed. Nicholas Lossky, 519. Geneva: WCC Publications, 2002.

Tavard, George. "'Hierarchia Veritatum' A Preliminary Investigation." *Theological Studies*, no.32 (1971): 278-289.

Twomey, Vincent. "'Hierarchy' of Truths." *The Furrow*, vol. 42, no. 9 (September, 1991): 500-504.

www.ingramcontent.com/pod-product-compliance
Lightning Source LLC
Chambersburg PA
CBHW062002040426
42447CB00010B/1867